Pride of
the Bears

By the Same Author

Pride of the Lions
Pride of the Jocks

Writing as Derek Beaugarde

2084: The End of Days

Pride of
the Bears

The untold story of the men and
women who made the Barça Bears

Derek Niven

Corkerhill Press

Published in 2020 by Corkerhill Press

Copyright © Derek Niven 2020

Derek Niven has asserted his right to be identified as the author of this
Work in accordance with the Copyright, Designs and Patents Act 1988

Front cover illustrations by Wheech © 2020

ISBN Paperback: 978-0-9935551-6-9
ebook: 978-0-9935551-7-6

A CIP catalogue copy of this book can be found at the British Library
in London and the National Library of Scotland.

Published with the help of Indie Authors World
www.indieauthorsworld.com

IndieAuthors
World

For my lovely grandson Cailean John Murphy

ACKNOWLEDGEMENTS

The author wishes to acknowledge the valued assistance of Indie Authors World partners Sinclair and Kim Macleod in the publishing of this book. As always, I would like to thank Gillian Murphy for her expert editorial skills. A special thanks to my old railway colleagues John Steele, the DJ, and a big Rangers fanatic, who always takes a keen interest in promoting my books, and Robin Dale, who initially encouraged me to 'kick on' with the idea of the 'Pride' series. Also, thanks go to my brother James McGee, another staunch Rangers fan, who introduced me to Peter McCloy, Colin Stein and Willie Johnston in the Legends Lounge at Ibrox Stadium. Special thanks go to Nicky Neef and her mother Marcia for their memories of Gerry Neef.

For his unsurpassed genealogical knowledge of Banffshire, my thanks go to Bruce Bishop, an ASGRA member. Thanks to Iain Ferguson at National Records of Scotland for helping me with an Andy Penman record access issue during the 'coronavirus pandemic'. I did not foresee having to mention that phrase in the publication of this book. Kind thanks to Joyce Hunter, a descendant of the McEachans and MacDonalds of South Uist, for her background on Alex

MacDonald's ancestry. Also to the late Sir Dirk Bogarde for the pseudonym and our shared alumni of Allan Glen's School.

Finally, without the unswerving love, support and patience of my wife Linda, this 'Pride' series of books would never have seen the light of day.

WHY TEDDY BEARS?

Theodore Roosevelt, 26th President of the USA, on an unsuccessful hunting trip in 1902 in Mississippi, refused to shoot an old bear the trackers had tied to a willow tree for him to kill. He claimed this was unsportsmanlike and the myth of the 'Teddy Bear' was founded. The Steiff toy company in Germany heard of the story and they began making teddy bears for the global market.

In the mid-20th century fans of Glasgow Rangers Football Club latched on to this and used it as Glasgow rhyming slang for their club – the Teddy Bears. Rangers victorious 1972 European Cup Winners' Cup team in Barcelona were then nicknamed – the Barça Bears.

CONTENTS

PREFACE

Once again the casual reader may think this third book in the Pride series is about the beautiful game of football. On the contrary, this publication is once more about fickle fate and human destiny. This has been demonstrated no more clearly than by the current coronavirus pandemic, which as this book goes to press, is sweeping across the globe with devastating consequences. The ancestors of the Rangers players researched in this book also went through an even greater pandemic. Following the Armistice, millions of soldiers were demobilised and repatriated to their homes across the world and they took with them the Spanish Flu pandemic of 1918-19. Around 50 million people died of the flu, more than had been killed in WWI. Let us hope and pray that with scientific and medical technology the world does not have to mourn that dreadful number in the current pandemic.

This book researches the chance accumulation of fateful meetings and unions between men and women from the early 19th century, which culminated in the procreation of a remarkable group of young men, who wrote themselves into the history books almost half a century ago. It is about men and women who were born 40 years and more before the formation of a new association football club in 1872 in the district of Ibrox, in the parish of Govan, at that time still separated from the city of Glasgow, which eventually grew into the world-renowned Glasgow Rangers Football Club. These were people who were brought together by destiny, having no idea that one day their descendants would be immortalised over a hundred years after their births in the early 19th century.

Almost exactly a century after the formation of the club, on a warm evening on 24 May 1972, in the Camp Nou Stadium in Barcelona, a team of 15 young Scotsmen and one young German, playing for Glasgow Rangers, created Scottish footballing history by beating the Russian side Dinamo Moscow by 3-2 to lift the European Cup Winners' Cup. They were the first Scottish club side to lift this prestigious trophy. The legend of the Bears of Barcelona, otherwise known as the Barça Bears, was born.

The Camp Nou has a humorous place in the author's heart. He and his great railway colleague DJ Steeley used to run quiz nights for the railway Finance team in McConnell's Bar in Hope Street, Glasgow, near their Buchanan House HQ. One of the questions, which had been plucked from some quiz book was: "Where in Spain is the Camp Nou stadium?" At the end of the quiz, the author announced the answer as Madrid, which was published in the book. Personnel colleague Ross Dickson came charging across, bellowing: "No effing way is the Camp Nou in Madrid. It's in Barcelona! I know, cos I was there!"

The Rangers team picked to play that evening were all Scottish-born boys from predominantly working-class backgrounds. The only exception to this was the German-born substitute goalkeeper Gerry Neef. Another feature which the book will reveal is the Barça Bears were almost exclusively products of or came through at a young age, that tough period of austerity and rationing just a few short years after World War II.

Whether that instilled a steely toughness which they carried on towards Barcelona is a matter of conjecture. Certainly instilled into the ethos of the young Rangers team at that time was their great desire to emulate the feat of their greatest rivals Celtic and achieve European glory. Celtic had lifted the European Cup five years previously in 1967 in Lisbon. The Rangers backroom staff under manager Willie Waddell and ex-British Army assistant Jock Wallace would have drummed this into the team picked to play in the Camp Nou final in 1972.

Looking at the exorbitantly paid international players developed nowadays at Barcelona, Real Madrid, Chelsea, Manchester United, Bayern Munich and Paris St Germain football clubs, who compete for the major European trophies, it can be quickly realised that never again will teams of working-class lads ever be able to win such coveted awards. Billions are now spent in trying to wrest Europe's most sought after awards. Indeed, Rangers spent countless millions in the Sir David Murray era to try and put the club back into the top echelons of Europe. It led the club towards liquidation and almost ended its long and illustrious history. The current pandemic has shone an unflattering light on the modern-day financially driven professional football clubs and their players and world football will need to carefully examine itself once this coronavirus has been conquered.

In 2022 the Barça Bears will celebrate the 50th anniversary of their landmark victory and it is possible that, by then, the club will have risen, under new manager Stephen Gerrard, like the Phoenix from the ashes of the financial turmoil of the early 21st century. Much will be retold about the famous victory in the Camp Nou in 1972. All of that detail, eagerly awaited by Rangers fans around the globe, including the goal by Colin Stein, followed by two goals from Willie Johnston, will be written, much more succinctly than this author, by authors and sports journalists who are footballing men. Their books will also elaborate on the causes of the crowd trouble at the end of the game, which became known as the 'Battle of Barcelona', due to celebrating fans spilling on to the pitch and clashing with over-zealous Spanish riot police.

The author is, instead, a professional genealogist and member of the Association of Scottish Genealogists (ASGRA). The reader may ask what brought a professional genealogist to want to write the family history of the Barça Bears. My father Archie was an ardent Rangers supporter and I think he wanted me to follow the Teddy Bears. To that end, on 26 November 1969, my father walked me the mile and a half from our home in Corkerhill Railway Village to Ibrox Park to watch Rangers face Polish side Gornik Zabrze in a European Cup Winners' Cup second leg match. Rangers were trailing 3-1 from the first leg, but there was great optimism that manager Davie White's side would easily overcome that score in the return match on home turf. The fans' optimism was dispelled that damp evening as Rangers were beaten by another 3-1, going down 6-2 to Gornik. The defeat ended Davie White's managerial career, but as my father and

I trudged despondently back from Ibrox Park to Corkerhill, Archie uttered, "I'll never be back at Ibrox again."

Although I have a copy of the match programme, given to me on my retirement from the rail industry in 2007, it seems to serve as a reminder of my father's dismissive words and that Rangers was not the team for me at that point in my young life. However, five of the Rangers players on that miserable, damp evening went on to win ECWC medals less than three years later in Barcelona; goal scorers Colin Stein and Willie Johnston, captain John Greig and substitutes Gerry Neef and Andy Penman. Although Davie White's career ended abruptly at Rangers, in hindsight, he had constructed the nucleus of players who marched on to Barcelona, and he deserves great credit for this.

Celtic at that time continued to be in the ascendency in Scottish football. They were on course for a new record-breaking 'nine-in-a-row' league championship titles and another final appearance in the European Cup against the Dutch team Feyenoord in 1970. I decided that Celtic was the team I wanted to support. My father, a Protestant, had no objections, although probably deep down he would rather have seen me go to Ibrox. Two of my younger brothers, James and David, went on to become ardent Rangers supporters. My late mother Margaret, although raised a Roman Catholic, was also a big Teddy Bears fan, along with my sisters Jessie and Margaret. I was the only one to follow the Hoops.

However, it was the support for Celtic, dating back to 1967, that kindled within my soul the idea for a series of books celebrating the family histories of famous Scottish footballing heroes. The first book in the series published in 2017 was

Pride of the Lions. The book sets out to celebrate the 50th anniversary of the Lisbon Lions not from a footballing perspective, but a genealogical, familial, religious and social history perspective. The second book in the series, published in 2018, was Pride of the Jocks. This book sets out to celebrate the 16 greatest Scottish football managers, such as Busby, Shankly, Stein and Ferguson, again from the perspective of the men and women who made them in a genealogical sense.

Three Rangers managers are covered in Pride of the Jocks; Willie Waddell, Jock Wallace and Graeme Souness, the first two being the managerial architects of the 1972 success. Of course, many Rangers aficionados will argue that the legendary Bill Struth deserves a chapter, however, he was before the author's time and the truly modern footballing era. This third book in the series, Pride of the Bears, tells the family histories of the men and women who procreated the Rangers team that won the European Cup Winners' Cup in 1972.

The books serve to show that even in greatness we are, as we say in Scotland, "a' Jock Tamson's bairns". My family history is a tale of poor, struggling agricultural labourers, coal miners and railway workers striving to achieve more than their working-class existences afforded them. Within my history are tales of struggles through two great wars, tales of illegitimacy, infant mortality, the poorhouse and grinding poverty. The average reader will be able to associate their family history in the same vein.

Likewise, the genealogy of the Barça Bears reveals a remarkably similar story of ordinary working-class boys from predominantly poor backgrounds who went on to achieve something extraordinary. The reader should be aware that it has not been possible to research every aspect of the lives of the ancestors of the Bears and in the main, the detailed research concentrates on their Scottish family history. One player, reserve goalkeeper Gerry Neef, being a German, has no Scottish ancestry at all, although, he did marry a Scottish lass. Also, some of the heroes of Barcelona have now passed on to that great stadium in the sky, but the book will not dwell on their passing. Thus, the Barça Bears will remain immortal, even within the confines of this book.

The Barça Bears.

This is their amazing story.

Part 1

The Barça Bears players
24 May 1972

Camp Nou, Barcelona, Spain

CHAPTER 1

Peter McCloy (Goalkeeper)

Honours as a Rangers player:
1 European Cup Winners' Cup
2 Scottish League titles
4 Scottish Cups
4 Scottish League Cups

The young Peter McCloy

Peter Allwell Lyon McCloy was born on 26 November 1946 at Grangeston Cottage, Girvan, Ayrshire, to father James McCloy, a factory caretaker, and mother Mary Lyon. He is a retired professional goalkeeper who played for Motherwell and Rangers. Peter McCloy was a member of the Rangers team which won the 1972 Cup Winners' Cup, and was Rangers first-choice goalkeeper for most of his 16-year spell at the club, despite competition from players such as Gerry Neef, Stewart Kennedy and Jim Stewart.

McCloy, the son of a former professional footballer, his father James had played for St Mirren, joined Motherwell from Crosshill Thistle in 1964. He stayed there for six seasons before joining Rangers in a player exchange deal in 1970. At Ibrox, he was nicknamed 'The Girvan Lighthouse', due to his birthplace and the fact he stood at 6 foot 4 inches tall. He played under three different Rangers managers: Willie Waddell, Jock Wallace, in both of his spells as manager, and John Greig. He won multiple honours in his Rangers career, including two Scottish League titles, four Scottish Cups, four Scottish League Cups and the 1972 European Cup Winners' Cup. He was one of only five players who featured in every match of the European campaign, alongside Sandy Jardine, Willie Mathieson, Alex MacDonald and Colin Stein. He made 535 appearances in all competitions for Rangers and played for Scotland on four occasions.

After retiring as a player in 1986, McCloy went into coaching, firstly during the Graeme Souness era as Rangers manager, until 1988. He went on to work with several clubs and goalkeepers including Andy Goram and Jim Leighton. McCloy was on the bench for Hearts during both legs of their 1988-89 UEFA Cup tie against Bayern Munich.

Peter's parents - James McCloy and Mary McGilp Lyon
Peter's father James McCloy was born on 12 October 1906 at Kilmony Cottages, Lochwinnoch, Renfrewshire, to father James McCloy, a cloth beetler, and mother Helen Stokes. In 1911, James, 4, resided at Back Row, Kilnknowe Cottages, Lochwinnoch, with his father James McCloy, 35, a beetler in a bleach works, mother Ellen, 30, and his other siblings. As a young man, James became a professional footballer, starting in the junior ranks with Petershill. He signed for the 'Bully Wee' Clyde making only 2 appearances before transferring to

St Mirren in Paisley and playing from 1933-1938. He played 148 times for the Buddies and appeared in the 1934 Scottish Cup final. He also had a short spell with Bradford City in 1938-39, playing 37 times in the league and had 1 FA Cup appearance. In May 1939 he moved to Swansea Town but never played for the club, as his career was interrupted by the outbreak of WWII.

In the winter of 1916, a month after the end of the terrible Battle of the Somme, which claimed half a million casualties amongst the British and Allied forces, Peter's mother Mary McGilp Lyon was born on 28 December 1916 at 11 Dean Road, Kilbirnie, Ayrshire, to father John Lyon, a police constable, and mother Isabella Allwell. The family resided at 1 New Street, Stevenston during WWI. After leaving school Mary became a hairdresser.

James McCloy, 28, a professional footballer, of 28 Kilnknowe Cottages, Howwood, Lochwinnoch, married Mary McGilp Lyon, 20, a hairdresser, of Roselea, Shore Road, Stevenston, on 7 July 1937 at Ardeer Church of Scotland. The wedding was conducted by Rev Samuel White, minister of Ardeer Church; the best man was Henry McCloy, James's brother, and the best maid was Mary McGilp Kane, Mary's cousin. James and Mary had two known sons; John Lyon (b. November 1937, Stevenston) and Peter Allwell Lyon (b. 16 November 1946, Girvan). In 1938 the McCloy family moved to Yorkshire and James played for a short spell with Bradford City. In 1939 James transferred to Swansea Town, however, he did not play for the club as his spell there was interrupted by the war. After WWII ended the McCloy family moved back to Ayrshire and son Peter Allwell Lyon McCloy was born on 16 November 1946 at Grangeston Cottage, Girvan. At that time James was working as a factory caretaker.

Peter's paternal grandparents – James McCloy and Helen Stokes

Peter's paternal grandfather James McCloy was born on 5 February 1875 in Coleraine, County Coleraine, Ulster, Ireland, to father David McCloy, a cloth beetler, and mother Sarah Jane Duff. James may have been raised in Londonderry, County Derry and he was brought up in the Presbyterian Church. After schooling, James became a cloth beetler in the textile industry. A beetler operated a beetling machine, used in the textile industry as part of the finishing process, such as, with linen. The cloth would be pounded with heavy weights to flatten and close up the threads, thereby producing a sheen.

Peter's grandmother Helen Stokes, aka Ellen or Nellie, was born around 1881 in England to Irish-born father Joseph Stokes, a labourer, and mother Jane Shearer. James McCloy and Helen Stokes married in Belfast, County Antrim, Ireland around 1899 and they had seven known children, although one unidentified child died in infancy; David (b. ~1900, Belfast), Andrew (b. ~1902, Belfast), James (b. 12 October 1906, Lochwinnoch), Jennie (b. ~1909, Ireland), Ellen (b. ~1911, Lochwinnoch) and youngest son Henry. In 1901, James McCloy, 25, a labourer in a bleach works, resided in Hillview Street, Whiteabbey, Belfast, County Antrim, with wife Nellie, 21, and son David, 11 months old.

Around 1905, the family migrated to Scotland and they lived in Lochwinnoch, Renfrewshire. Son James McCloy was born on 12 October 1906 at Kilmony Cottages, Lochwinnoch. It appears that Nellie was back in Ireland in 1909 when she gave birth to daughter Jennie.

In 1911, James McCloy, 35, a beetler in a bleach works, resided at Back Row, Kilnknowe Cottages, Lochwinnoch, with wife Ellen, 30, children David, 10, at school, Andrew, 9, at school, James, 4, Jennie, 2, and Ellen, less than one-month-old. Also boarding there was James's Irish-born brother David McCloy, 29, also a beetler in a bleach works. Helen McCloy nee Stokes, 71, wife of James McCloy, a retired textile worker, died on 1 May 1952 at 28 Kilnknowe Cottages, Howwood, of coronary thrombosis. James McCloy, 90, a retired cloth beetler, of 52 Wallace Avenue, Elderslie, died on 21 January 1966 at Riccartsbar Hospital, Paisley, of bronchopneumonia and arteriosclerosis.

Peter's maternal grandparents – John Lyon and Isabella Allwell

Peter's maternal grandfather John Lyon was born on 20 March 1890 at Redburn, Colmonell, Ayrshire, to father Thomas Lyon, a mason, and mother Janet Thom. After schooling, John became a police constable with the Ayrshire Constabulary. Peter's maternal grandmother Isabella Allwell was born on 3 February 1891 at Redheugh, Kilbirnie, Ayrshire, to father Peter Allwell, a coachman domestic servant, and mother Mary McGilp. John Lyon, 26, a police constable, residing at the Constabulary Station, Dalry, married Isabella Allwell, 24, a net worker, of Dean Road, Kilbirnie, on 10 November 1916, during WWI, at Isabella's home. The wedding was conducted by Rev R K Goodfellow, minister of United Free Church of Scotland; the best man was James Jamieson and the best maid was Janet Allwell, Isabella's sister.

John and Isabella had a known daughter; Mary McGilp (b. 28 December 1916). Mary McGilp Lyon was born on 28 December 1916 at 11 Dean Road, Kilbirnie, Ayrshire. John Lyon, a police constable, and his wife Isabella Lyon nee Allwell were both still alive and living at Roselea, Shore Road, Stevenson, in 1937.

Peter's paternal great-grandparents – David McCloy and Sarah Jane Duff

Peter's paternal great-grandfather David McCloy and his great-grandmother Sarah Jane Duff were born around 1850 in County Coleraine, Ulster, Ireland. David, a cloth bee-tler, and Sarah had two known sons in Ireland; James (b. 5 February 1875, Coleraine) and David (b. ~1882). David McCloy, a cloth beetler, and wife Sarah Jane McCloy nee Duff were both recorded as deceased by 1966.

Peter's paternal great-grandparents – Joseph Stokes and Jane Shearer

Peter's other paternal great-grandfather Joseph Stokes (or Stoke) and his great-grandmother Jane Shearer were born around 1855 and they were of Irish descent. However, Joseph, a labourer, and Jane were living in England when they had a known daughter Helen, aka Ellen or Nellie (b. ~1881). Joseph Stokes, a labourer, and wife Jane Stokes nee Shearer were both deceased by 1952.

Peter's maternal great-grandparents – Thomas Lyon and Janet Thom

Peter's maternal great-grandfather Thomas Lyon was born on 6 April 1852, in Colmonell, Ayrshire, to father Alexander Lyon, a fisherman, and mother Jane McWhirter. After schooling, Thomas became a joiner and later a stonemason. Peter's great-grandmother Janet Thom was born on 17 September 1867, in Maybole, Ayrshire, to father Duncan Thom, an iron miner, and mother Jane Edgar. Soon after her birth, the family moved to Waterside, Dalmellington in the Doon valley. After schooling, Janet went into domestic service.

Thomas Lyon, 37, a joiner, of Redburn, Colmonell, Ayrshire, married Janet Thom, 21, of Waterside, Dalmellington, on 28 December 1888 at 39 Truffhill, Waterside. The wedding was conducted by Rev George S Hendrie, minister of Dalmellington Parish Church; the best man was James Moore and the best maid was Agnes Thom, Janet's sister. Son John Lyon was born on 20 March 1890 at Redburn, Colmonell. Thomas Lyon, a mason, was deceased by 1916, but his wife Janet Lyon nee Thom was still alive by then.

Peter's maternal great-grandparents – Peter Allwell and Mary McGilp

Peter's other maternal great-grandfather Peter Allwell was born around 1856, in Ireland, to father Peter Allwell, an estate gardener, and mother Mary Wilson. After schooling, Peter became a ploughman. Peter's great-grandmother Mary McGilp was born around 1854, in Argyllshire, to father Archibald McGilp, a shepherd, and mother Janet Gillies. Like many girls in the Victorian era, Mary went into domestic service and she was employed at Eastfield House, Rothesay on the Isle of Bute. Between 1853 and 1864 the proprietor of Eastfield House was Mr McFarlane Esquire and at the time the house was described as: *"A fine dwelling house with garden and some ornamental ground attached."*

Peter Allwell, 19, a ploughman, of Kerry Conlin, Kingarth, Isle of Bute, married Mary McGilp, 22, a domestic servant, of Eastfield House, Rothesay, Isle of Bute, on 27 May 1875 at 48 Ladeside Street, Rothesay. The wedding was conducted by Rev Patrick Wood Minto, minister of Inverurie Free Church; the best man was William Faulds and the best maid was Janet McFarlane. The Rev Patrick Wood Minto later transferred to minister the Scots Church in Cannes, south of France, dying on 7 March 1914 and buried in the Cimitière du Grand Jas, Cannes.

Peter and Mary had two known daughters in Ayrshire; Isabella (b. 3 February 1891) and Janet. Daughter Isabella Allwell was born on 3 February 1891 at Redheugh, Kilbirnie, and at that time Peter was working as a coachman in domestic service. Redheugh House is now a Category B listed building on the register of British Listed Buildings. During

WWI Peter worked in one of the many munitions factories in Ayrshire. Peter Allwell, a munitions worker, and wife Mary Allwell nee McGilp were still alive in 1916.

Peter's great-great-grandparents – Alexander Lyon and Jane McWhirter

Peter's maternal great-great-grandfather Alexander Lyon (or Lyons) and his great-great-grandmother Jane McWhirter were born around 1820, in Ayrshire. Alexander Lyon married Jane McWhirter on 11 September 1842 as recorded in their respective parishes of Girvan and Colmonell. Alexander, a fisherman, and Jane had three known children in Colmonell; Thomas (b. 6 April 1852), Elizabeth McConnochie (b. 16 June 1857) and Mary McWhirter (b. 4 November 1860). Alexander Lyon, a fisherman, and wife Jane Lyon nee McWhirter were still alive in 1888.

Peter's great-great-grandparents – Duncan Thom and Jane Edgar

Peter's other maternal great-great-grandfather Duncan Thom and his great-great-grandmother Jane Edgar were both born around 1835 in Ayrshire. Duncan Thom, an iron miner, married Jane Edgar on 7 June 1867 in Maybole, Ayrshire. Duncan and Jane had six known children; in Maybole, Janet (b. 17 September 1867); and in Dalmellington, Mary Bell (b. 11 March 1869), John (b. 14 March 1871), Jeanie (b. 24 December 1872), Agnes Cron (b. 6 August 1874) and Maggie (b. 9 July 1881).

Around 1868, Peter moved his family to Waterside, Dalmellington, and he worked as an iron miner for the Dalmellington Ironworks, which at that time was extensively mining ironstone and coal and producing pig iron for the burgeoning Industrial Revolution. The period of the 1870s in Dalmellington was known as the time of the 'Big Money'. The price of iron ore and coal had soared and workers were making double their normal wages, although there was a corresponding slump in the following decade. Duncan Thom, an iron miner, and wife Jane Thom nee Edgar were both still alive in 1888.

Peter's great-great-grandparents – Peter Allwell and Mary Wilson

Peter's other maternal great-great-grandfather Peter Allwell and his great-great-grandmother Mary Wilson were born around 1825, in Ireland. Peter, an estate gardener, and Mary had a known son Peter (b. ~1856) in Ireland. Peter Allwell, an estate gardener at Redheugh, Kilbirnie, was dead by 1875, however, his wife Mary Allwell nee Wilson was still alive by then.

Peter's great-great-grandparents – Archibald McGilp and Janet Gillies

Peter's other maternal great-great-grandfather Archibald McGilp and his great-great-grandmother Janet Gillies were born around 1825, in Argyllshire. Archibald McGilp married Janet Gillies on 16 September 1850 in the parish of Dunoon and Kilmun, Argyllshire. Archibald, a shepherd, and Janet had three known daughters; Isabella (b. 20 March 1853, Rhu, Dunbartonshire), Mary (b. ~1854, Rhu) and Janet (b. 15 September 1860, Cumlodden, Argyllshire). Archibald McGilp, a shepherd, and wife Janet McGilp nee Gillies were still alive in 1875.

CHAPTER 2

Sandy Jardine (right back)

Honours as a Rangers player:
1 European Cup Winners' Cup
3 Scottish League titles
5 Scottish Cups
5 Scottish League Cups

The young Sandy Jardine

The elder of twin boys by five minutes, William Pullar Jardine was born at 11.50 am on Hogmanay, 31 December 1948 at the Western General Hospital, Edinburgh, to father James Jardine, a bus driver, and mother Margaret Perry Pullar. Just five minutes later his twin brother James Ross Jardine followed William into the world. At that time the family were living at 50 Grove Street, Edinburgh, Midlothian. Jardine was a professional footballer, who played for Rangers and Hearts, and also represented Scotland. Although his name was William he became widely known as Sandy due to his fair hair.

Jardine grew up near Tynecastle Park, the home ground of Hearts, who he avidly supported as a boy. His ability at football shone through at an early age, earning local and national schoolboy honours with Balgreen Primary and

Tynecastle Secondary Schools. As a youth, he played for North Merchiston Boys Club, United Crossroads Boys Club and Edinburgh Athletic. He also trained at the Hearts' training ground, although it was many years later before he played for his beloved team.

Jardine signed for Rangers in 1964 as a midfielder and after a couple of years in the reserves, he made his debut, aged 18, in a 5-1 league win at home to Hearts on 4 February 1967, playing at right-half. This match took place a week after Rangers had been infamously knocked out of the Scottish Cup by player-manager Jock Wallace's lowly Berwick Rangers. He scored his first Rangers goal a few weeks later on 18 March 1967 in a league match against Ayr United. That same season, Jardine played in the 1967 European Cup Winners' Cup Final against Bayern Munich, with Rangers losing 1-0 after extra time.

Jardine played in various defensive positions, becoming a regular under manager Davie White, even playing centre-forward, before finally settling as a right full-back at the start of the 1970-71 season under new manager Willie Waddell. He proved a revelation at right-back and was a strong player who enjoyed marauding forward. He won his first major trophy in 1970, beating Celtic 1-0 in the Scottish League Cup Final.

The following season he was an ever-present in the Rangers side which reached the 1972 Cup Winners' Cup Final, one of only five players who featured in all eight matches en route to the final. He scored the first goal of a two-nil win over Bayern Munich in the semi-final. Jardine went on to help Rangers win the final, defeating Dinamo Moscow 3-2 at the Camp Nou. Between 27 April 1972 and 30 August 1975, he did not miss a single game for Rangers and played in 171 consecutive matches for them. In 1974-75, he helped Rangers win their first Scottish league title in 11 years. Jardine was a key part of Rangers campaigns that won the domestic treble in 1975-76 and 1977-78. He twice won the Scottish Football Writers Association Player of the Year award.

By the early 1980s Rangers were in decline, and 33-year-old Jardine was reluctantly given a free transfer to Hearts in mid-1982 by manager John Greig. Greig allowed Jardine to leave due to his long service and his stated wish to end his playing career at the Edinburgh club he supported as a boy.

The Rangers legend, Ally McCoist, recalled in Sandy's biography: *"Dignity is the quality that epitomises Sandy best and he displayed it every day during his struggle against illness. Despite his pain, he was even able to return to Ibrox to unfurl the league flag. It was a proud moment for Sandy and I know he was also touched when the club decided to name the Govan Stand in his honour."*

Sandy's parents - James Jardine and Margaret Perry Pullar

Sandy's father James Jardine was born on 3 October 1920 at 11 Stewart Terrace, Dalry and Gorgie, Edinburgh, to father William Jardine, a heating engineer, and mother Mary Ross. Sandy's mother Margaret Perry Pullar was born on 19 April 1914 at 6 Thistle Place, Morningside, Edinburgh, to father William Pullar, a coal salesman, and mother Margaret Mennelaws.

James Jardine, 27, a motor bus driver, of 4 Hutchison View, Edinburgh, married Margaret Perry Pullar, 33, a biscuit factory worker, of 50 Grove Street, Edinburgh, on 14 February 1948 at the Church of St John the Evangelist. The wedding was conducted by Fr David B Porter, rector of St John the Evangelist Episcopal Church; the witnesses were William and Ann Pullar, Margaret's brother and sister, also of 50 Grove Street.

James and Margaret had twin sons William Pullar and James Ross (b. 31 December 1948). William Pullar Jardine was born at 11.50 am on 31 December 1948 at the Western General Hospital, Edinburgh, and twin brother James Ross Jardine was born at 11.55 am. At the time James and Margaret were living at 50 Grove Street, Edinburgh and they brought their family up in the Gorgie district close to Tynecastle Park, the home of Heart of Midlothian.

Sandy's paternal grandparents – William Jardine and Mary Ross

Sandy's paternal grandfather William Jardine was born on 10 December 1894 at 110 Gorgie Road, Gorgie, Edinburgh, to father James Jardine, a stonemason, and mother Marion Lithgow. His grandmother Mary Ross was born around 1894 in Edinburgh to father Finlay Ross, a brewery cooper, and mother Margaret Smith. Mary Ross married her first husband surnamed Young and he was probably killed during WWI. Mary was certainly a widow by 1920 when she met William Jardine. At that time, Mary worked in the Castle Mills factory of the North British Rubber Company, founded in 1857, in Fountainbridge, Edinburgh. It was one of the biggest employers in Edinburgh and during WWI it was churning out wellington boots, pneumatic tyres and rubber fabric for dirigible balloons.

William Jardine, 25, an engineer's labourer, of 110 Gorgie Road, Edinburgh married Mary Young or Ross, 26, a widowed rubber worker, of 11 Stewart Terrace, Edinburgh on 16 April 1920 at 122 Bonnington Road, Leith. The wedding was conducted by Rev Robert S McClelland, minister of St Cuthbert's Parish Church of Scotland; the best man was George C Alexander and the best maid was Marion Lithgow Jardine, William's sister.

Son James Jardine was born on 3 October 1920 at 11 Stewart Terrace, Dalry and Gorgie, Edinburgh. William Jardine, a mechanical engineer, and his wife Mary Jardine, previously Young, nee Ross were both still alive and living in Edinburgh in 1948.

Sandy's maternal grandparents – William Pullar and Margaret Laidlaw Menelaws

Sandy's maternal grandfather William Pullar was born around 1890 in Edinburgh to father David Pullar, a coal merchant, and mother Agnes McWilliam. After schooling, William also became a coal salesman. Sandy's maternal grandmother Margaret Laidlaw Menelaws (or Mennelaws) was born on 26 July 1892 at 26 Ponton Street, Edinburgh to father James Menelaws, a brewer's assistant, and mother Elizabeth Laidlaw.

William Pullar, 21, a coal salesman, married Margaret Menelaws, 20, a rubber worker, both of 16 Upper Grove

Place, Edinburgh on 25 August 1911 at 6 Murieston Road, Edinburgh. The wedding was conducted by Rev Andrew M Smith, minister of Bruntsfield United Free Church; the best man was Joseph Man and the best maid was Margaret G Pirie. William and Margaret had three known children; William, Margaret Perry (b. 19 April 1914) and Ann. Daughter Margaret Perry Pullar was born on 19 April 1914 at 6 Thistle Place, Morningside, Edinburgh. William Pullar, a rubber mill worker at the North British Rubber Company, was still alive in 1948, however, his wife Margaret Laidlaw Pullar nee Menelaws was dead by then.

Sandy's paternal great-grandparents – James Jardine and Marion Lithgow

Sandy's paternal great-grandfather James Jardine was born around 1865 in Lochmaben, Dumfriesshire to father David Jardine, a carter, and mother Elizabeth Paxton. His great-grandmother Marion Lithgow was born around 1865 in Hamilton, Lanarkshire to father Robert Lithgow, a lathe worker, and mother Janet Stewart. James Jardine, 26, a mason, married Marion Lithgow, 26, a domestic servant, both of 150 Dundee Street, Dalry, Edinburgh, on 3 July 1891 at 34 Blacket Place, Edinburgh. The wedding was conducted by Rev W Whyte Smith DD, minister of Newington Free Church of Scotland; the best man was Robert Ballantyne and the best maid was Agnes Lithgow, Marion's sister. James and Marion had five known children in Gorgie, Edinburgh; David (b. ~1892), Robert (b. ~1893), William (b.

10 December 1894), Marion Lithgow (b. ~1897) and James (b. ~1900). In 1901, James Jardine, 35, a mason, resided at 110 Gorgie Road, Edinburgh, with wife Marion, 35, children David J, 9, a scholar, Robert, 7, a scholar, William, 6, a scholar, Marion, 4, a scholar, and James, 1. James Jardine, a mason, and wife Marion were both still alive in 1920 and living in Gorgie, Edinburgh.

Sandy's paternal great-grandparents – Finlay Ross and Margaret Smith

Sandy's other paternal great-grandfather Finlay Ross, a brewery cooper, was born around 1865 in Edinburgh and his great-grandmother Margaret Smith was also born around 1865 in Edinburgh and they had a known daughter Mary (b. ~1894). Finlay Ross, a brewery cooper, and his wife Margaret were both dead by 1920.

Sandy's maternal great-grandparents – David Pullar and Agnes McWilliam

Sandy's maternal great-grandfather David Pullar, a coal merchant, and his great-grandmother Agnes McWilliam were both born around 1865 and they had a known son William (b. ~1890) in Edinburgh. David Pullar, a coal merchant, and wife Agnes were both still alive in 1911 and living in Morningside, Edinburgh.

Sandy's maternal great-grandparents – James Menelaws and Elizabeth Laidlaw

His other maternal great-grandfather James Menelaws was born on 8 October 1849 in West Port, St Cuthbert's, Edinburgh to father George Menelaws, a labourer, and mother Agnes Heron. As a boy, James was raised as a Roman Catholic and he was baptized in January 1852 in St Mary's RC Cathedral in the Saint Andrew's district of Edinburgh's New Town.

His great-grandmother Elizabeth Laidlaw was born around 1856 in Dalkeith, Midlothian, to father William Laidlaw, a butcher, and mother Violet Walkinshaw. James Menelaws, 22, a brewer's servant, married Elizabeth Laidlaw, 17, both of 23 Ponton Street, Dalry, Edinburgh, on 3 July 1873. The wedding was conducted by Rev W Tasker, minister of the Free Church of Scotland; the best man was Peter Buchanan and the best maid was Emily McLoan. James and Elizabeth had nine known children in Ponton Street; Violet (b. ~1875), George (b. ~1876), William (b. ~1878), James (b. ~1880), Alexander (b. ~1882), Agnes (b. ~1884), Georgina (b. ~1888), Lilian (b. ~1890) and Margaret (b. 26 July 1892).

In 1891, James Menelaws, 42, a distillery worker, resided in the same close as his mother Agnes still at 23 Ponton Street, Edinburgh, with wife Elizabeth, 32, children Violet, 16, a comb maker, George, 15, a blacksmith's apprentice, then William, 13, James, 11, Alexander, 9, Agnes, 7, all scholars, Georgina 3, and Lilian, 3 months old. James Menelaws, a work's stoker, was deceased by 1911, although, his wife Elizabeth was still alive then.

James's occupation as a work's stoker in a distillery is almost certainly associated with the famous Haig's whisky.

The Lochrin Distillery was built by James Haig (1755-1833) in 1780 in the area that is now the convergence of Ponton Street, Thornybauk and West Tollcross. A 'steam engine', probably stoked by James Menelaws, was a circular structure nearby located on land identified as belonging to 'Mr Haig' and linked to the distillery. Field Marshal Douglas Haig, 1st Earl Haig, Commander in Chief on the Western Front during WWI was the son of John Richard Haig of Haig & Haig Whisky Distillers.

Sandy's paternal great-great-grandparents – David Jardine and Elizabeth Paxton

Sandy's paternal great-great-grandfather David Jardine was born around 1840 in Dumfriesshire and his great-great-grandmother Elizabeth Paxton was born about the same time. David and Elizabeth had a known son James (b. ~1865) in Lochmaben, Dumfriesshire. David Jardine, a carter, was still alive in 1891, although, his wife Elizabeth was dead by then.

Sandy's paternal great-great-grandparents – Robert Lithgow and Janet Stewart

His other great-great-grandfather Robert Lithgow was also born around 1840 in Hamilton, Lanarkshire and his great-great-grandmother Janet Stewart was born about the same time. Robert and Janet had two known daughters in Hamilton; Marion (b. ~1865) and Agnes. Robert Lithgow, a lathe turner, was dead by 1891, although, his wife Janet was still alive then.

Sandy's maternal great-great-grandparents – George Menelaws and Agnes Heron

On Sandy's maternal line his great-great-grandfather George Menelaws and his great-great-grandmother Agnes Heron were born around 1830 in St Cuthbert's, Edinburgh. George and Agnes had a known son James (b. 8 October 1849) in West Port, St Cuthbert's, Edinburgh. The Menelaws family were Roman Catholic and son James was baptized in January 1852 in St Mary's RC Cathedral as recorded in CPRs as follows:-

> *CPR Births St Mary's Cathedral*
>
> *1849: James: Lawful: West Port: George Menelaws: Agnes Heron: born 8th October 1849: baptized January 1852: Sponsor Catherine Hunt: Priest William Mackay*

George Menelaws, a labourer, was dead by 1891, although, wife Agnes was still alive by then. In 1891, Agnes Menelaws, 49, a mangle keeper, resided up the same close as her son James at 23 Ponton Street, St Cuthbert's, Edinburgh, taking in a couple of boarders Eliza Pevay, 25, and Celia Duffy, 18, both paper mill workers.

Sandy's maternal great-great-grandparents – William Laidlaw and Violet Walkinshaw

His other maternal great-great-grandfather William Laidlaw and great-great-grandmother Violet Walkinshaw were born around 1835. William and Agnes had a known daughter Elizabeth (b. ~1856). William Laidlaw, a butcher, and wife Violet were both still alive in 1873.

CHAPTER 3

Willie Mathieson (left-back)

Honours as a Rangers player:
1 European Cup Winners' Cup
1 Scottish Cup

The young Willie Mathieson

Although born and brought up in Fife, Willie Mathieson has a surprising historical link to Govan, the home of his club Glasgow Rangers. The day after the Allies first bombed the Nazi-occupied city of Rome, William Mathieson was born on 20 July 1943 at 50 Balgriggie Park, Cardenden in Fife to father Andrew Mathieson, a coal miner stripper, and mother Margaret Skinner Wilson. In his youth, he played for St Andrews United and after leaving school he worked in the local Dundonald colliery as an apprentice electrician. He played in the left-back position for Rangers, amongst other clubs, and was nicknamed 'Wan Fit' due to his propensity for being exclusively left-footed. In admission, he stated: *"that my right foot was only good for standing on."* Mathieson spent fifteen seasons at Rangers from 1960 to 1975 and was involved in the club's historic 1972 European Cup Winners' Cup-winning team in Barcelona. He was one of only five players who played in every round of the 1971-72 campaign.

He played in over 300 games for Rangers, including the 1973 Scottish Cup final winning side over Celtic, made famous by Tam Forsyth's scuffed two-yard winning goal. In 1969 Mathieson represented the Scottish League gaining his only cap. He transferred to Arbroath in the 1975-76 season, playing 25 league games and then moved on to Raith Rovers for a final season. After retiring as a player he joined the Berwick Rangers coaching staff, working under former teammate Dave Smith. At that time Berwick won the Second Division championship, which was their first-ever trophy.

Willie's parents – Andrew Mathieson and Margaret Skinner Wilson

On 2 February 1915, an obscure incident occurred during WWI in Canada. German saboteur Werner Horn tried to blow up the Vanceboro Railway Bridge on the Canada-US border. That same day Andrew Mathieson was born at 48 Dundonald Den, Cardenden, Fife to father William Mathieson, a coal miner, and mother Elizabeth McGregor. After leaving school Andrew followed his father down into the bowels of the Fife coalfields.

Willie's mother Margaret Skinner Wilson was born on 13 January 1923 at Bankhead, Thornton, Kirkcaldy to father Alexander Hay Wilson, a cattle attendant at Bogie Mains Farm, Kirkcaldy, and mother Annie Dewar. Margaret's family later moved to Torbain Farm. This farm was formerly part of the large estate of Raith Park, which was to give its name to the local team Raith Rovers, where Willie spent a season playing. On the farm stood a 19th-century folly, Torbain Tower, a square crenellated tower on high ground, at the foot of Broom Hill and now a ruin.

Andrew Mathieson, 26, a coal miner stripper, of 28 Dundonald Crescent, Cardenden, married Margaret Skinner Wilson, 18, a cloth factory worker, of Torbain Farm, Kirkcaldy, on Hogmanay, 31 December 1941, during WWII, at Auchterderran Parish Church. The wedding was conducted by Rev Donald M Douglas; the best man was Robert Mathieson, Andrew's brother, and the best maid was Helen Arnott. Their son William was born on 20 July 1943, during WWII, at 50 Balgriggie Park, Cardenden, Fife.

Willie's paternal grandparents – William Mathieson and Elizabeth McGregor

Willie's paternal grandfather William Mathieson was born as William Mathewson on 12 April 1875 at Dundonald Colliery, Auchterderran, Fife to father William Mathewson, a coal miner, and mother Margaret Campbell. In 1881, William, 5, a scholar, still resided at Dundonald Colliery with his parents William and Margaret and his siblings. Willie's paternal grandmother Elizabeth McGregor was born around 1880 in Fife to father Alexander McGregor, a ploughman, and mother Elizabeth Anderson.

William Mathieson, 25, a coal miner, of Dundonald, Auchterderran, married Elizabeth McGregor, 20, a domestic servant, of Hyndloup, Auchterderran, on 20 April 1900 at the Manse, Auchterderran. The wedding was conducted by Rev A McNeil Houston, minister of Auchterderran Church of Scotland; the witnesses were D Fleming and D MacGregor. William and Elizabeth's son Andrew Mathieson was born on 2 February 1915, during WWI, at 48 Dundonald Den, Cardenden in Fife. In 1941, during WWII, William Mathieson, a coal miner, and his wife Elizabeth McGregor were still alive by then.

Willie's maternal grandparents – Alexander Hay Wilson and Annie Dewar

Willie's maternal grandfather Alexander Hay Wilson was born on 27 July 1884 in the Back Lands, Sinclairtown, Dysart in Fife to father John More Wilson, a carting contractor, and mother Margaret Black. In 1891, Alexander, 6, a scholar, resided at 223 St Clair Street, Dysart, with his parents John and Margaret. Willie's maternal grandmother Annie Dewar was born around 1888 in Fife to father George Dewar, an electrical engineer, and mother Ann Heaton.

Alexander Hay Wilson, 23, a ploughman, of Bogwells Farm, Dysart, married Annie Dewar, 22, an outdoor worker, of 165 Park Road, Gallatown, Kirkcaldy, on 18 February 1910 at 35 George IV Bridge, Edinburgh in a civil ceremony by warrant of the Sheriff Substitute of Lothians and Peebles. The witnesses were James Stark Nash, a coal miner, and Annie Halkett, a pottery worker. Their daughter Margaret Skinner Wilson was born on 13 January 1923 at Bankhead, Thornton, Kirkcaldy. At that time Alexander was a cattle attendant at Bogie Mains Farm, Kirkcaldy. Alexander Hay Wilson, a ploughman, and his wife Annie were still alive in December 1941, during WWII.

Willie's paternal great-grandparents – William Mathewson and Margaret Campbell

Willie's paternal great-grandfather William Mathewson (or Mathieson) was born on 22 June 1845 at Auchterderran, Fife to father John Mathewson, an agricultural labourer, and mother Janet Younger. His great-grandmother Margaret Campbell was born on 11 November 1849 in Auchterderran to father Andrew Campbell, a coal miner, and mother Margaret Rankine. William Mathewson, 21, a coal miner, married Margaret Campbell, 18, a pithead worker, both of Dundonald, Auchterderran, on 6 January 1868 at the Manse, Auchterderran. The wedding was conducted by Rev Patrick MacGregor Grant, minister of Auchterderran Parish Church; the best man was Henry Moyes and the best maid was Janet Campbell, Margaret's sister.

William and Margaret had six known children at Dundonald Colliery, Auchterderran; John (b. ~1868), Margaret, (b. ~1871), Andrew (b. ~1873), William (b. 12 April 1875), Janet (b. ~1878) and David (b. ~1880). In 1881, William Mathieson, 35, a coal miner, resided at Dundonald Colliery, with wife Margaret, 31, children John, 13, Margaret, 10, Andrew, 8, William, 5, all scholars, Janet, 3, and David, 3 months old. William Mathieson, a coal miner, was deceased by 1900, although his wife Margaret Campbell was still alive then.

Willie's paternal great-grandparents – Alexander McGregor and Elizabeth Anderson

Willie's other paternal great-grandfather Alexander McGregor, a ploughman, and his great-grandmother Elizabeth Anderson were born around 1855 in Fife. Alexander and Elizabeth had a known daughter Elizabeth (b. ~1880). Alexander McGregor, a ploughman, was deceased by 1900, although his wife Elizabeth was still alive then.

Willie's maternal great-grandparents – John More Wilson and Margaret Black

Willie's maternal great-grandfather John More Wilson was born around 1850 in Carnbee, Fife to father Alexander Wilson, a ploughman, and mother Lyall Wilson. In 1861, John, 10, a scholar, resided at Drumtenant Cotters, Collessie with his parents Alexander and Lyall. His great-grandmother Margaret Black was born illegitimately around 1844 in Elie, Fife to father James Black, a baker, and mother Margaret Skinner. In 1851, Margaret Black, 5, a scholar, resided at Bowhouse, Fife with her unmarried mother Margaret Skinner, 30. By 1880 Margaret had moved from Fife to Harmony Row, Govan and she was working as a domestic servant.

Just eight years earlier, in 1872, the Glasgow Rangers Football Club was founded and in 1899 the club moved to

Ibrox Park, Govan and by a twist of fate, the young Willie Mathieson followed the same path to Govan, when he signed for Rangers over 80 years after Margaret's birth. Harmony Row FC in Govan is a community club formed in 1915 and the club's patron is Sir Alex Ferguson, who also played alongside Willie Mathieson at Rangers.

John More Wilson, 30, a carting contractor, of 103 Mid Street, Pathhead, Fife, married Margaret Black, 34, a domestic servant, of 28 Harmony Row, Govan, on 24 June 1881 at 4 Woodville Place, Govan. The wedding was conducted by Rev Allan Cameron, minister of the Free Church of Scotland; the best man was Thomas Thomson and the best maid was Helen Anderson. John and Margaret had a son Alexander Hay Wilson born on 27 July 1884 in the Back Lands, Sinclairtown, Dysart in Fife.

In 1891, John M Wilson, 40, a contractor, resided at 223 St Clair Street, Dysart, with wife Margaret, 44, son Alexander, 10, a scholar, and servant Maggie Pratt, 20, a dairymaid. By the turn of the 20th century, John turned his hand to farming and he tenanted at Carberry Farm in Dysart. In 1901, John Wilson, a farmer, resided at Carberry Farm, with wife Margaret, 54, his mother Lyall, 74, and a visitor Janet McMillan, 64, a gardener's widow. John More Wilson, 58, a farmer at Carberry Farm, Dysart, died on 29 November 1908 in Kirkcaldy Hospital, Sinclairtown of heart disease. His wife lived on to a good age and Margaret Wilson nee Black, 95, died on 13 January 1939 at Torbain Farm, near Kirkcaldy, of senility and adenitis.

Willie's maternal great-grandparents – George Dewar and Ann Heaton

Willie's other maternal great-grandfather George Dewar was born in Fife around 1860 and his great-grandmother Ann Heaton was born about the same time. George and Ann had a daughter Annie (b. ~1888). In 1910, George, an electrical engineer, and wife Ann Heaton were still alive and living in Kirkcaldy.

Willie's paternal great-great-grandparents – John Mathewson and Janet Younger

Willie's paternal great-great-grandfather John Mathewson and his great-great-grandmother Janet Younger were born around 1820 in Fife. John and Janet had a son William (b. 22 June 1845) at Auchterderran, Fife. The birth is recorded in the OPRs for the parish of Auchterderran as follows:-

> *OPR Births Auchterderran 405/2/203*
> *1845: Mathewson: William to John Mathewson &*
> *Janet Younger born on the 22nd June*

John Mathewson, an agricultural labourer, was dead by 1868, although his wife Janet was still alive by then.

Willie's paternal great-great-grandparents – Andrew Campbell and Margaret Rankine

His other great-great-grandfather Andrew Campbell and his great-great-grandmother Margaret Rankine were also born around 1820 in Fife. Andrew and Margaret had two known daughters; Margaret (b. 11 November 1849) and Janet in Auchterderran, Fife. Margaret's birth is recorded in the OPRs for the parish of Auchterderran as follows:-

OPR Births Auchterderran 405/2/27

1849: Campbell: Margaret to Andrew Campbell & Margaret Rankine on the 11th November

Andrew Campbell, a coal miner, and wife Margaret were both still alive in 1868.

Willie's maternal great-great-grandparents – Alexander Wilson and Lyall Wilson

Willie's maternal great-great-grandfather Alexander Wilson and his great-great-grandmother Lyall Wilson were both born around 1827, Alexander in Leven and Lyall in Pathhead in Fife. Alexander and Lyall had a son John More (b. ~1850, Carnbee). In 1861, Alexander Wilson, 34, a ploughman, resided at Drumtenant Cotters, Collessie, with wife Lyall, 34, and son John, 10, a scholar. Alexander Wilson, a carting contractor, was still alive in 1881, but dead by 1901. In 1901, Lyall Wilson, 74, a farmer's widow, resided at Carberry Farm, Dysart, with her son John, 50, a farmer, and daughter-in-law Margaret, 54.

Willie's maternal great-great-grandparents – James Black and Margaret Skinner

Willie's other great-great-grandfather James Black was born about 1820 in Culross, Clackmannanshire and his great-great-grandmother Margaret Skinner was born around 1821 in Cupar, Fife. James and Margaret had an illegitimate daughter Margaret (b. ~1844, Elie). It appears they never married and, in 1851, James Black, 30, a baker, resided in High Street, Kirkcaldy, with wife Ann, 34, and 2 baker's apprentices James Thomson, 18, and George Aitken, 15. At the same time unmarried Margaret Skinner, 30, resided in Bowhouse, Fife, with daughter Margaret Black, 5, a scholar. James Black, a baker, and Margaret Skinner were both dead by 1881.

CHAPTER 4

John Greig MBE

(Captain and defender)
Honours as a Rangers player:
1 European Cup Winners' Cup
5 Scottish League titles
6 Scottish Cups
5 Scottish League Cups

The young John Greig

The day after the RAF carpet-bombed the Germany industrial city of Düsseldorf, John Greig was born on 11 September 1942 at 26 Clearburn Crescent, Prestonfield, Edinburgh, one of six children, to father Thomas Greig, a boot warehouseman, and mother Agnes Anderson Black and he was named after his grandfather. Of his early years, Greig stated: *"Britain was at war. However, I have no memories of those dark days other than the air raid shelter that remained in our back garden for years after and which became a favourite play area for me and my pals"*. Greig played mainly as a defender and spent his entire professional career with Rangers, as a player, manager and director.

Greig played his youth football with United Crossroads in Edinburgh, under the supervision of Eric Gardner, and he supported Hearts as a boy. Bob McAuley signed Greig for Rangers and despite his initial reluctance to move to the Ibrox club, Greig did as advised by his father Thomas. John Greig, 24, a professional footballer, still at 26 Clearburn Crescent, when he was married on 27 March 1967 at Canongate Church, Edinburgh.

A determined, forceful player, recognised for his great leadership qualities, Greig made 755 official appearances for Rangers; including 498 in the league, 72 in the Scottish Cup, a club record 121 in the League Cup, and 64 in European tournaments. He scored 120 goals for the club and won three domestic trebles. Greig started his career with Rangers as a forward, before being moved back to midfield – playing initially alongside another Rangers legend, Jim Baxter – and finally to left-back.

Greig was captain when Rangers won the European Cup Winners' Cup in 1972 beating Dinamo Moscow 3-2 in Barcelona. Although he had an enormously successful playing career, his captaincy coincided with a period of sustained success for Rangers' Old Firm rivals, Celtic, under Jock Stein, from the late 1960s until the mid-1970s. Greig's fortitude during that period further cemented his reputation as one of Rangers most celebrated captains, being given the nickname 'Captain Courageous'.

Greig played for Scotland on 44 occasions, 15 as captain, between 1964 and 1971. He scored the late winner in Scotland's 1-0 victory against Italy at Hampden Park on 9 November 1965 and in 1967 achieved the distinction of captaining the Scottish side who beat the newly-crowned World Champions England 3-2 at Wembley Stadium. The author's father Archie was at that game, which included Jim Baxter famously playing keepie-uppie to taunt the England team. Greig also represented the Scottish League on 13 occasions.

Greig's playing career ended in May 1978 when he was appointed manager of Rangers, replacing Jock Wallace. The club failed to win the league championship during Greig's time as manager, finishing no higher than second-place achieved in 1978-79. Greig's team won two Scottish Cups and two League Cups during his five full seasons as manager. Greig fell under intense pressure from the Scottish media, Rangers supporters and the club's directors and he resigned in October 1983, replaced by the returning Jock Wallace. Greig was voted 'The Greatest Ever Ranger' in 1999 by the club's supporters and he has a statue erected outside the Main Stand at Ibrox Stadium.

John's parents – Thomas Greig and Agnes Anderson Black
John's father Thomas Greig, aka Tam, was born on 11 October 1898 at 2 Simpson's Court, Potterrow, Edinburgh to father John Greig, a brewer's labourer, and mother Margaret Paterson. John's mother Agnes Anderson Black was born on 10 December 1900 at Kilduff Mains, Athelstaneford, Haddingtonshire to father Adam Richardson Black, a ploughman, and mother Jessie Anderson Bell. In 1911, Thomas, 12, at school, resided in Potterrow, Edinburgh with his father John Greig, 54, a scavenger for Edinburgh town council, his mother Margaret, 51, and his siblings.

Thomas Greig, 23, a boot warehouseman, of 75 Buccleuch Street, St Bernard, Edinburgh, married Agnes Anderson Black,

21, a fruiterer's shop assistant, of 9 Buccleuch Street, St Bernard, Edinburgh, on 7 July 1922 at 6 Bellevue Terrace, Edinburgh. The wedding was conducted by Rev G W Dalgleish, minister of Martyrs & St John's United Free Church of Scotland; the best man was Alfred Greig, Thomas's brother, and the best maid was Helen Bell, Agnes's cousin, of Dolphingstone, Tranent.

The district of St Bernard's was once home to Edinburgh's 'third' football team, St Bernard's FC. Formed from the Third Edinburgh Rifle Volunteers FC in 1878 their main home ground was the Royal Gymnasium Stadium, 'the Gymmie', and they were part of the 'Edinburgh Slam' of 1895 when Heart of Midlothian won the Scottish League championship, Hibernian won the Second Division championship and St Bernard's lifted the Scottish Cup beating Renton 2-1 at Ibrox Stadium. In the year John Greig was born St Bernard's played their last game on 16 May 1942, a 3-2 home defeat to East Fife. It was 'mothballed' for the remainder of WWII, and after being forced to sell the Royal Gymnasium ground to settle a debt, the club was wound up.

Thomas and Agnes had six children named by Greig as *"Four boys Alfie, Alex, Tam and me [John], and two girls, Nessie and Margaret. Tam, the third youngest of six, was like a second father and he spent hours encouraging me to develop what [footballing] skills I had been blessed with"*. Son John Greig was born on 11 September 1942, during WWII, at 26 Clearburn Crescent, Prestonfield, Edinburgh. Thomas, a boot warehouseman, and Agnes were still living at Clearburn Crescent in 1967 when their son John married.

John's paternal grandparents – John Greig and Margaret Paterson

John's paternal grandfather John Greig was born illegitimately on 18 November 1857 at Skinner's Close, St Giles, Edinburgh to mother Helen Greig, a book folder. His grandmother Margaret Paterson (or Patterson) was born around 1860 in Edinburgh to father Thomas Paterson, a tailor, and mother Sarah Jack. John Greig, 40, a shop porter, married Margaret Paterson, 36, a domestic servant, who signed with her 'x' mark, both of No.2 Simpson's Court, Potterrow, Edinburgh, on 14 August 1896 at St Columba's Episcopal Church in Scotland, Johnston Terrace, Edinburgh. The wedding was conducted by Fr H H Willmott, the priest in charge; the best man was James White and the best maid was Wilhelmina White.

John and Margaret had four known children in Edinburgh; John (b. ~1896), Mary (b. ~1897), Thomas (b. 11 October 1898) and Alfred (b. ~1901). Son Thomas Greig was born on 11 October 1898 at 2 Simpson's Court, Potterrow, Edinburgh to father John Greig, a brewer's labourer, and mother Margaret Paterson. In 1911, John Greig, 54, a scavenger for Edinburgh town council, resided in Potterrow, Edinburgh with wife Margaret, 51, children John, 16, also a scavenger, Mary, 14, Thomas, 12, and Alfred, 10, both at school. John Greig, a retired City Cleansing Department scavenger, and his wife Margaret Greig nee Paterson were both still alive in 1922 and living in Edinburgh.

John's maternal grandparents – Adam Richardson Black and Jessie Anderson Bell

John's maternal grandfather Adam Richardson Black was born around 1872 in Haddington to father Alexander Black, a farm servant, and mother Jane Richardson. His grandmother Jessie Anderson Bell was born around 1875 in Haddington to father Henry Bell, a cattleman, and mother Agnes Anderson. Adam Richardson Black, 28, a ploughman, married Jessie Anderson Bell, 25, an outdoor worker, both of Kilduff Mains, Athelstaneford, Haddingtonshire, on 16 February 1900 at the Manse, Haddington. The wedding was conducted by Rev William Broadfoot, minister of the Church of Scotland; the best man was John Bell, Jessie's brother, and the best maid was Joanna Grierson. Daughter Agnes Anderson Black was born on 10 December 1900 at Kilduff Mains, Athelstaneford, Haddingtonshire.

Kilduff Mains was the home farm for the Kilduff Estate. The mansion house, a Category B listed building, was built by John Home (1722-1808) the dramatist and minister who was given the lease of Kilduff by Sir David Kinloch in 1767. Robert Adam added wings in 1770, later rebuilt. Adam Richardson Black, a ploughman, was deceased by 1922, however, his wife Jessie was still alive at that time.

John's paternal great-grandmother – Helen Greig

John's paternal great-grandmother Helen Greig, aka Ellen, was born around 1831 in Edinburgh. Helen Greig, a book folder, gave birth to son John Greig illegitimately on 18

November 1857 at Skinner's Close, St Giles, Edinburgh. No father of repute has been identified. Ellen lived a life of grinding poverty and she gave birth to another illegitimate son Joseph Greig in 1870. The following year in 1871 Ellen, 36, a general servant, was an inmate in the Craiglockhart Poorhouse with her son Joseph, only 7 months old.

Helen Greig never married and she continued to work as a domestic servant, still living in Edinburgh in 1896. Ellen Greig, 76, a single woman, died on 23 April 1907 in the Craiglockhart Poorhouse, Colinton, Edinburgh of cardiac failure as registered by Dr E A Robertson MD. James Smith, the assistant governor, who registered Ellen's death was unaware of her parents' names. Ellen died in ignominious circumstances in the poorhouse; little knowing her great-grandson would go on to have a statue erected to him at Ibrox Stadium as 'Captain Courageous'.

John's paternal great-grandparents – Thomas Paterson and Sarah Jack

John's other paternal great-grandparents Thomas Paterson and Sarah Jack were both born around 1830 in Edinburgh. Before 1858 Sarah Jack was married to a first husband surnamed Johnston. Thomas Paterson, a tailor, married Sarah Johnston nee Jack in 1858 in the district of St Giles and they had a daughter Margaret (b. ~1860) in Edinburgh. Thomas Paterson, a tailor, and his wife Sarah were both dead by 1896.

John's maternal great-grandparents – Alexander Black and Jane Richardson

John's maternal great-grandparents Alexander Black and Jane Richardson were both born around 1845 in Haddingtonshire. Alexander Black, a farm servant, married Jane Richardson and they had a known son Adam Richardson (b. ~1872). Alexander and wife Jane were both still alive in 1900.

John's maternal great-grandparents – Henry Bell and Agnes Anderson

His other maternal great-grandparents Henry Bell and Agnes Anderson were also born around 1845 in Haddingtonshire. Henry Bell, a cattleman, married Agnes Anderson and they had two known children; John and Jessie Anderson (b. ~1875). Henry and wife Agnes were also both still alive in 1900.

CHAPTER 5

Derek Johnstone (Centre forward)

Honours as a Rangers player:
1 European Cup Winners' Cup
3 Scottish League titles
5 Scottish Cups
5 Scottish League Cups

The young Derek Johnstone

Derek Joseph Johnstone was born on 4 November 1953 at 31 Finella Place, Dundee, Angus, one of seven sons, to father Ronald Johnstone, a charge-hand carpet backer, and mother Emily Elizabeth Perry Hughson. He is a former professional footballer and manager and he played mainly for Rangers during his career. He generally played as a striker, but could play in central defence, and also in midfield. Johnstone signed for Rangers as a schoolboy in 1968. He turned professional in 1970, making his debut on 19 September 1970, aged 16 years and 319 days. In that debut, Johnstone scored two goals in a 5-0 victory against Cowdenbeath.

Just five weeks later, Johnstone famously thrust himself into the limelight when his header secured a 1-0 victory over rivals Celtic in the Scottish League Cup final of 1970-71. Willie Waddell had surprised young Derek with a set of tickets for the game. The whole of the Johnstone clan came down from Dundee to watch him play at Hampden for his first cup final in a bus nicknamed *"the DJ Special"*. Despite his heroics against the Parkhead side, Johnstone found regular first-team outings in the No.9 jersey hard to come by, largely due to the presence of Colin Stein. He compensated for his lack of frontline action by often playing as a centre-back, usually when Ronnie McKinnon and Colin Jackson were injured. When the duo was ruled out of the European Cup Winners' Cup final in 1972, Johnstone, still only 18, deputised at centre-half in the victorious match against Dinamo Moscow.

Johnstone soon became a first-team regular, and he picked up a Scottish Cup winners' medal in 1973 when Rangers defeated Celtic 3-2 at Hampden Park. He eventually picked up a league championship medal at the end of the 1974-75 campaign, as Rangers ended Celtic's nine-in-a-row reign, and he was an integral part of the Gers treble success a year later. In 1977-78 Rangers won their second treble inside three years. Johnstone was the outstanding performer, scoring 38 goals during the campaign, and he was awarded Scottish Football Writers' Player of the Year.

In 1978 he was named club captain, and in his first season as captain, Johnstone lifted the Scottish Cup, scoring twice in the final's second replay against Hibernian, and he also won the League Cup. However, that season was to be the high-water mark for the John Greig era and Rangers' fortunes nosedived spectacularly thereafter. They did win the Scottish Cup in 1981 and the Scottish League Cup in 1982, but they found themselves playing second fiddle in the Premier Division to Celtic and the emerging New Firm of Alex Ferguson's Aberdeen and Jim McLean's Dundee United.

Having been placed on the transfer list by Greig in April 1983, Johnstone left Rangers after the Scottish Cup Final defeat against Aberdeen to join Chelsea. Signed in September 1983, Johnstone provided extra cover in the Chelsea squad which won the Second Division title in 1984. He failed to hold down a regular place and he had a month on loan to Dundee United during the 1983-84 season. He was tempted back to Ibrox by Jock Wallace in January 1985. He returned to a Rangers side that was in the midst of a doleful period in their history. It was hoped that the return of a former hero could galvanise an ailing team. It failed to work and Johnstone was handed a free transfer when Graeme Souness took over the reins at Ibrox in the summer of 1986. Johnstone had a brief stint in management at Partick Thistle and he is now a sports pundit.

Derek's parents – Ronald Johnstone and Emily Elizabeth Perry Hughson

Derek's father Ronald Johnstone was born on 20 September 1919, less than a year after the Armistice, at 179 Blackness Road, Dundee, to father Joseph Johnstone, a locomotive fireman, and mother Jane Macintyre. Although a railwayman by trade, his father Joseph had at that time not been demobbed from the army and was still serving as a Private in the Labour Corps. With Joseph on active service, the birth was registered by Ronald's mother Jane. Derek's mother Emily Elizabeth Perry Hughson was born on 19 July 1924 at 19 Graham Street, North Leith, Edinburgh to father Magnus William Hughson, a general labourer, and mother Catherine Dailly.

By the outbreak of WWII, in the town of Dundee, known for 'jute, jam and journalism', Ronald was working as a jute calenderer when he met his first wife Christina, the daughter of Edward Short, and a jute mill overseer. A calenderer operated a rolling machine used to press and finish the woven jute fabric. Ronald Johnstone, 20, of 179a Blackness Road, Dundee married Christina Jamieson McIntosh Short, 20, both jute calenderers, of 16 Wellgrove Street, Lochee, Dundee, on 30 March 1940. The wedding was conducted by Fr William C Gow, curate of St Mary Magdalene's Episcopal Church; the best man was Robert Butchart, Ronald's step-brother, and the best maid was Margaret Short, Christina's sister.

When she married Christina was pregnant, however, just a few months after the wedding, tragedy struck. Christina Jamieson McIntosh Johnstone, 21, died on 22 August 1940 in Maryfield Hospital, Dundee of chronic endocarditis and pericarditis, death under gas and oxygen during a Caesarean section as certified by Dr Peter Kinnear MB ChB. The following was recorded in a Register of Corrected Entries:-

> *"Cause of Death: sudden heart failure during anaesthesia administered for a necessary operation. Chronic endocarditis aggravated by a state of pregnancy: Dr James Ferguson, Dundee. Procurator Fiscal's Office, Dundee, 1/10/1940 (Signed) D J Henry, Procurator Fiscal. 2nd October 1940 at Dundee Norman Steele, Registrar."*

The following year in September 1941, Ronald lost his mother Jane Johnstone, who also died in Maryfield Hospital, and it was not until 1943 that Ronald remarried his second wife. Ronald Johnstone, 23, a widowed general labourer, of 179a Rosefield Place, Dundee, married Emily Elizabeth Perry Hughson, 18, a jute reeler and winder, of 15 Mid Kirk Style, Dundee, on New Year's Day, 1 January 1943 in St Mark's Church of Scotland, Dundee. The wedding was conducted by Rev J Victor Logan; the best man was Charles McGuckin and the best maid was Mary Keenan. Son Derek Joseph Johnstone was born on 4 November 1953 at 31 Finella Place, Dundee, to father Ronald, a charge-hand carpet backer, and mother Emily.

Johnstone's final memories of his father in 1964 were:

> *"Dad was a foreman in the Tay Bridge Jute Mills in Dundee. He was a grafter, a proud man who tried his damnedest to provide for his family. Across a period of twenty years, Ronald Johnstone had fathered seven sons with my mum Emily and the Johnstone clan was a tight unit. We were never awash with money but we got by as he battled against serious asthma. As he endured another health problem, I made the journey from Fintry Primary to Dundee Royal Infirmary faithfully every night. I may have been just ten but letting dad know he was never far from my thoughts was always so important to me. As I turned into the ward, I saw that his bed lay empty. I was too young to recognise the nurse's silent commiseration. I headed home. Mum realised I had been to the hospital and had found a newly, unmade bed. 'Your dad has passed*

away, Derek.' I was the last person to see my forty-six-year-old dad alive".

Derek's paternal grandparents – Joseph Johnstone and Jane Macintyre

Derek's paternal grandfather Joseph Johnstone was born illegitimately on 7 November 1884 at Chapel Street Cottage, Portsoy, Banffshire, to father James Joseph Johnstone, a tailor journeyman, of Seafield Street, Portsoy, and mother Elsie Helen Paterson, a feuar's daughter. His grandmother Jane Macintyre (or McIntyre) was born on 2 December 1879 at 49 North Back Street, Canongate, Edinburgh, to father John McIntyre, a mason's labourer, and mother Jane Cumming. Jane moved to work in the jute mills of Dundee where she met her first husband Robert Mill Butchart.

Jane Macintyre, 22 a jute spinner, of 10 Well Road, Dundee, married Robert Mill Butchart, 27, a wood sawyer, of 85 Liff Road, Lochee, on 28 October 1904. The wedding was conducted by Rev Andrew N Sutherland, minister of McCheyne Memorial United Free Church; the best man was David Butchart, Robert's brother, and the best maid was Mary Ann Ritchie. Jane and Robert had a son Robert Butchart. However, Jane was widowed just a few weeks before the outbreak of WWI. Robert Butchart, 36, of 125 Roseberry Street, Dundee, died on 22 July 1914 in Dundee District Asylum, Liff, of general paralysis of the insane, as registered by his widow Jane Butchart of 13 Shepherd's Loan, Dundee.

Later that year, during WWI, Jane married second husband Joseph Johnstone. Joseph Johnstone, 30, a farm labourer, of 193 Blackness Road, Dundee, married Jane Butchart nee Macintyre, 33, a widowed jute spinner, of 175 Blackness Road, Dundee, on Hogmanay, 31 December 1914. The wedding was conducted by Rev Robert Pointer, minister of St Mark's Parish Church of Scotland; the best man was Alexander Macintyre and the best maid was Annie Macintyre, Jane's brother and sister. Joseph then got a job as a locomotive fireman in Dundee, most likely with the North British Railway Company. As the war rolled on Joseph was drafted into the British Army as a Private in the Labour Corps and he was still on active duty into 1919.

Son Ronald Johnstone was born on 20 September 1919 at 179 Blackness Road, Dundee to father Joseph Johnstone, a locomotive fireman, serving as a Private in the Labour Corps, and mother Jane Macintyre. In 1923 the plethora of railway companies was amalgamated into the 'Big Four' and the North British was subsumed into the London and North Eastern Railway Company. Joseph Johnstone, a railway stoker, by then with the LNER, was still alive in 1941, during WWII, at 179a Blackness Road, Dundee, when his wife Jane died. Jane Johnstone previously Butchart nee Macintyre, 61, died on 12 September 1941 at Maryfield Hospital, Dundee, of septicaemia, a septic ulcer and an injury to the right wrist as certified by Dr Philippa Gaffikin MB ChB. The death was registered by her son Robert Butchart.

Derek's maternal grandparents – Magnus William Hughson and Catherine Dailly

Derek's maternal grandfather Magnus William Hughson, aka William, was born around 1894 at Nation, North Delting, Shetland, and he is of Viking descent. His maternal grandmother Catherine Dailly was born around 1895 in Dundee. Magnus William Hughson, a general labourer, married wife Catherine Dailly on 27 April 1905 in Dundee. During WWI Magnus Hughson served as Rating L1291 in the Royal Naval Reserve. Daughter Emily Elizabeth Perry Hughson was born on 19 July 1924 at 19 Graham Street, North Leith, Edinburgh, to father Magnus William Hughson, a general labourer, and mother Catherine Dailly. Magnus and Catherine were still alive in 1943, during WWII.

Derek's paternal great-grandparents – James Joseph Johnstone and Elspeth Helen Paterson

Derek's paternal great-grandfather James Joseph Johnstone, aka James Forsyth Johnstone, was born illegitimately and registered as James Forsyth on 23 November 1855 at Mid Street, Keith, Banffshire, to mother Elizabeth Forsyth, 25, a domestic servant. James's 'father of repute' was later named as James Johnstone, a crofter, in Keith. His great-grandmother Elspeth Helen Paterson, aka Elsie, was born around 1860 in Banffshire. James, a tailor journeyman, of Seafield Street, Portsoy, and Elsie, a feuar's daughter, had a son Joseph Johnstone born illegitimately on 7 November 1884 at Chapel Street Cottage, Portsoy, Banffshire. However, James and

Elsie did not marry and James Forsyth Johnstone, a tailor journeyman, later married Margaret Ann Galt in 1900 in Huntly, Banffshire, and they had a son James Johnstone.

Elspeth Helen Paterson never married, although her son later recorded her incorrectly as Elsie Johnstone, and she was still alive in 1915, during WWI. James Forsyth Johnstone, 71, a retired tailor, married to Margaret Galt, died on 7 February 1927 at 179a Land Street, Keith, Banffshire, of a cerebral haemorrhage as certified by Dr John D Campbell MB. The death was registered by his son James Johnstone.

Derek's paternal great-grandparents – John Macintyre and Jane Cumming

Derek's other paternal great-grandfather John Macintyre (or McIntyre) was born on 16 December 1830 in Fort William, Kilmallie, Argyllshire to father Donald Macintyre, a drover, and mother Ann Cumming. His great-grandmother Jane Cumming was born around 1844 in Aberdeenshire to father Thomas Cumming, a shoemaker, and mother Sarah McPherson. John and Jane were 'cousins-german', meaning they were first cousins through the Cumming line and, although it was legal for first cousins to marry under Scots Law, it was not recommended for genetic health reasons.

John Macintyre, 26, an iron founder, married Jane Cumming, 16, who signed with her 'x' mark, both of 8 Seamount Place, Aberdeen, on 8 September 1860 at North Lodge, King Street, Aberdeen. The wedding was conducted by Rev John Wilson, minister of Aberdeen North Church of Scotland; the witnesses were Joseph Rose and Robert Gordon. John and Jane had three known children; Alexander, Annie and Jane (b. 2 December 1879). Daughter Jane Macintyre (or McIntyre) was born on 2 December 1879 at 49 North Back Street, Canongate, Edinburgh to father John McIntyre, a mason's labourer, and mother Jane Cumming. John Macintyre, a carter, was dead by 1904, although, wife Jane was still alive in 1915.

Derek's paternal great-great-grandparents – James Johnstone and Elizabeth Forsyth

Derek's paternal great-great-grandfather James Johnstone was born around 1825 in Banffshire. His great-great-grandmother Elizabeth Forsyth was born around 1827 in Keith, Banffshire, to father John Forsyth, an innkeeper, and mother Mary Russell. In 1841, Elizabeth, 14, resided at Mid Street, Keith, with her father John Forsyth, 40, a spirit dealer, her mother Mary, 45, and her siblings.

James Johnstone met Elizabeth Forsyth in early 1855 in Keith and she fell pregnant. Son James Joseph Johnstone, aka James Forsyth Johnstone, was born illegitimately as James Forsyth on 23 November 1855 at Mid Street, Keith, Banffshire to mother Elizabeth Forsyth, 25, a domestic servant. James Johnstone, a crofter, was later named as the 'father of repute', although he never married Elizabeth. Elizabeth Forsyth, 33, a washerwoman, who signed with her 'x' mark, married Alexander McKimmie, 29, a widowed hammerman, both of Mid Street, Keith, on 28 October 1865. The wedding was conducted by Rev Andrew Begg, assistant minister of Keith Parish Church of Scotland; the witnesses were William McKimmie, Alexander's brother, and Robert Burgess. James and Elizabeth were both dead by 1927.

Derek's paternal great-great-grandparents – Donald Macintyre and Ann Cumming

Derek's other paternal great-great-grandfather Donald Macintyre (or McIntyre) was born around 1800 in Kilmallie, Argyllshire, and his great-great-grandmother Ann Cumming (or Cumings) was born around 1800 in Old Machar, Aberdeenshire. Donald Macintyre had various occupations as a drover, a soldier, Chelsea Pensioner and a policeman. Fort William was a garrison town, its Gaelic name is *'an Gearasdan'* and Donald enlisted into the army at the fort. Donald Macintyre, in Banavie, Kilmallie, married Ann Cumming on 24 March 1828 in Fort William. The marriage is recorded in the OPRs for the parish of Kilmallie as follows:-

> *OPR Births Kilmallie 520/2/174*
> *1828: March 24: Donald McIntyre in Ban[a]vie &*
> *Ann Cumings*

Donald and Ann had a son John (b. 16 December 1830) in Fort William. The birth is recorded in the OPRs for the parish of Kilmallie as follows:-

> *OPR Births Kilmallie 520/2/85*
> *1830: John, son to Donald McIntyre, a drover Fort*
> *William, & Ann Cumming born the 16th December*
> *1830 baptized 19th*

A drover was a hardy agricultural worker whose job it was to drive sheep or cattle on foot to market in all weathers and conditions. Fort William was on the main drover's road to the meat markets in Glasgow's Gallowgate, much of which followed the old General Wade's military roads, constructed after the Jacobite defeat at the Battle of Culloden in 1746. The drover's road is still used today by tourists and hill walkers and is called the West Highland Way. Donald, a policeman in Aberdeen, and wife Ann were both dead by 1860.

Derek's paternal great-great-grandparents – Thomas Cumming and Sarah McPherson

Derek's other paternal great-great-grandparents Thomas Cumming and Sarah McPherson were born about 1810 in Old Machar, Aberdeenshire. Thomas Cumming and Ann Cumming above were almost certainly brother and sister. Thomas Cumming, a shoemaker, married Sarah McPherson on 30th December 1839 in Woodside, Old Machar. The marriage is recorded in the OPRs for the parish of Old Machar as follows:-

> OPR Marriages Old Machar 168/B/17/206
>
> 1839: Thomas Cumming, Shoemaker, Woodside, & Sarah McPherson there, both in this parish, signified their purpose of marriage, by Mr Alexander Rae, Elder, & being proclaimed, they were married on the 30th December 1839 by the Revd Robert Forbes Minister of Woodside

Thomas and Sarah had a daughter Jane (b. ~1844). Jane married her 'cousin-german' John Macintyre in 1860 and her father Thomas, a shoemaker foreman, and mother Sarah was still alive then.

Derek's paternal great-great-great-grandparents – John Forsyth and Mary Russell

Derek's paternal great-great-great-grandfather John Forsyth was born on 3 May 1798 in Keith, Banffshire, to father William Forsyth, a butcher, and mother Isobel Grant. His great-great-great-grandmother Mary Russell was born about 1796 in Keith. In 1821 John Forsyth, an innkeeper, was censured for 'antenuptial fornication' by the Keith Kirk Session, almost certainly with Mary Russell as they married that same year. John and Mary and had seven known children in Keith; Isabella (b. 10 June 1821), William (b. 12 July 1822), Jane aka Jean (b. 11 August 1823), Janet (b. 24 April 1825), Elizabeth (b. ~1827), John (b. 29 February 1832) and James (b. ~1833). In 1822 John Forsyth purchased a lair for his aunt Margaret Grant. The lair was later displaced and Margaret's body was interred in the Forsyth Burial Aisle in Keith Parish Church.

In 1841, John Forsyth, 40, a spirit dealer, resided at Mid Street, Keith, with wife Mary, 45, children Isabella, 15, Jane, 15, Elizabeth, 14, John, 10, and James, 8. John was listed in the County Directory of Scotland in 1857 as 'Forsyth, John ~ Keith.' John Forsyth, 65, the innkeeper of the Black Bull Inn, died on 23 March 1863 at his inn on Mid Street, Keith of chronic bronchitis as certified by Dr A Turner MD, 'who saw him 20th March 1863'. The death was registered by son

James Forsyth, of Haughs Cairney, Keith. Mary Forsyth nee Russell was dead by 1865.

Derek's paternal great-great-great-great-grandparents – William Forsyth and Isobel Grant

Derek's paternal great-great-great-great-grandfather William Forsyth and great-great-great-grandmother Isobel Grant were born around 1770 in Keith, Banffshire. William Forsyth, a butcher, married Isobel Grant and they had a known son John (b. 3 May 1798) in Keith. Isobel also had an unmarried sister Margaret Grant who died in 1822 and who was interred in the Forsyth Burial Aisle in Keith Parish Church. William Forsyth, a butcher, and his wife Isobel Forsyth nee Grant were both dead by 1863.

CHAPTER 6

Dave Smith (left half)

Honours as a Rangers player:
1 European Cup Winners' Cup
1 Scottish Cup
1 Scottish League Cup

The young Dave Smith

The day after the Allied Expeditionary Force for the invasion of Nazi-occupied Europe was formed, David Bruce Smith was born on 14 November 1943 at 97 West North Street, Aberdeen, Aberdeenshire to father James Henry Smith, a shore labourer, and mother Margaret Collie Burness Baigrie. Smith had two brothers who were also professional footballers. Doug Smith spent his entire career with Dundee United, and Hugh Smith played for Forfar Athletic and Greenock Morton. Primarily a left-sided midfielder, Smith started his playing career for Aberdeen and he moved to Rangers in August 1966. During his time at Ibrox, he made 303 appearances winning the Scottish League Cup in 1971, the Scottish Cup in 1973 and, most notably, the

European Cup Winners' Cup in 1972. That same year, he was voted the Scottish Football Writers' Association Player of the year. During his career he collected two Scotland caps, featuring twice in friendly matches against the Netherlands.

Smith left Ibrox in November 1974 for Arbroath, where he took up a player-coach role. He went on to become player-manager at Berwick Rangers in 1976 and he transformed the club's fortunes, guiding them to the Scottish Second Division championship in 1979. He left Berwick in 1980 and subsequently managed Huntly, Gala Fairydean and Whitehill Welfare. Smith spent one close season during his career playing for Seattle Sounders and Los Angeles Aztecs in the North American Soccer League and he also played in South Africa.

Dave's parents – James Henry Smith and Margaret Collie Burness Baigrie

Dave's father James Henry Smith was born on 19 May 1907 at 94 Western Road, Woodside, Aberdeen, to father William Smith, an Aberdeen Corporation carter, and mother Margaret Barron. Dave's mother Margaret Collie Burness Baigrie was born on 30 March 1907 at 147 Constitution Street, St Nicholas, Aberdeen, to father Hugh Wallace Baigrie, a shore labourer, and mother Margaret Cruikshank Burness.

James Henry Smith, 27, a mental hospital attendant at the Royal Mental Hospital, Cornhill Road, Aberdeen, married Margaret Collie Burness Baigrie, 27, a confectioner's shop assistant, of 97 West North Street, Aberdeen on 27 December 1934 at 80 Spring Garden, Aberdeen. The wedding was conducted by Rev P C Millar, minister of West Church of Scotland, St Nicholas; the best man was Hector Will and the best maid was Helen Y Keith. James, a shore labourer, and Margaret had three known sons, all who became professional footballers; Doug, Hugh and David Bruce (b. 14 November 1943). Son David Bruce Smith was born on 14 November 1943, during WWII, at 97 West North Street, Aberdeen.

Dave's paternal grandparents – William Smith and Margaret Barron

Dave's paternal grandfather William Smith was born on 17 June 1869 at Ordie, Logie Coldstone, Aberdeenshire, to father William Smith, a carter, and mother Mary Simpson. His grandmother Margaret Barron was born around 1868 in Strathdon, Aberdeenshire to father William Barron, a mason journeyman, and mother Helen Findlay. In 1881, William, 11, a scholar, resided at No.4 Hamlet, Ordie, Logie Coldstone, with his widowed mother Mary Smith, 45, who '*knitts stockings &c*', sister Margaret, 14, a scholar, and brother John, 8.

William became a railway carter with the North British Railway Company and Margaret went into domestic service. William Smith, 29, a railway carter, of Bucksburn, Newhills, married Margaret Barron, 30, a cook domestic servant, of Goval Bank, St Machar, on 10 June 1898 at the Northern Hotel, Kittybrewster. The wedding was conducted by Rev J T Cox, minister of Dyce Parish Church of Scotland; the best man was John Topp and the best maid was Helen F Barron, Margaret's sister.

William and Margaret had two known sons in Woodside, Aberdeen; William Barron (b. ~1900) and James Henry (b. 19 May 1907). In 1901, William Smith, 31, an Aberdeen Corporation carter, resided at 16 Queen Street, Woodside, Aberdeen, with wife Margaret, 33, and son William B, 1. Son James Henry Smith was born on 19 May 1907 at 94 Western Road, Woodside, Aberdeen. William, a corporation carter, and wife Margaret were both dead by 1934.

Dave's maternal grandparents – Hugh Wallace Baigrie and Margaret Cruikshank Burness

Dave's maternal grandfather Hugh Wallace Baigrie (or Bagrie) was born around 1879 in Aberdeenshire to father William Baigrie, a scavenger, and mother Mary Wallace. His grandmother Margaret Cruikshank Burness was born around 1880 in Aberdeenshire to father Alexander Burness, a marine stoker, and mother Maggie Collie. Hugh Wallace Baigrie, 21, a shore labourer, of 113 West North Street, Aberdeen, married Margaret Cruikshank Burness, 20, a flax mill worker, of 119 West North Street, Aberdeen, on 13 July 1900 in the Trades Hall, Belmont Street, Aberdeen. The wedding was conducted by Rev John Damean, minister of Trinity Longe Congregational Church; the best man was James Watt Mearns and the best maid was Bella Baigrie, Hugh's sister. Daughter Margaret Collie Burness Baigrie was born on 30 March 1907 at 147 Constitution Street, St Nicholas,

Aberdeen. Hugh, a shore labourer, and wife Margaret were both still alive in 1934 in Aberdeen.

Dave's paternal great-grandparents – William Smith and Mary Simpson

Dave's paternal great-grandfather William Smith was born on 9 December 1822 in Monellie, Forgue, Aberdeenshire to father William Smith, a labourer, and mother Margaret Smith. His great-grandmother Mary Simpson was born around 1836 in Aboyne, Aberdeenshire to father Robert Simpson, a farmer, and mother Ann Milne. William Smith, an agricultural labourer, of Muir of Ordie, Logie Coldstone, married Mary Simpson, 27, of Mullich Cottage, Aboyne, on 4 August 1866 at 33 Union Place, Aberdeen. The wedding was conducted by Rev John Wilson, minister of Aberdeen North Church of Scotland; the witnesses were John Cameron and Peter Smith, William's brother.

This puts Rev John Wilson in a unique position, as six years earlier on 8 September 1860, he also married Derek Johnstone's great-grandparents John Macintyre and Jane Cumming. By sanctioning those two unions six years apart, Rev John Wilson could not have known he had set in motion the events that would procreate two of the Barça Bears.

William, a carter, and Mary had three known children in Logie Coldstone; Margaret (b. ~1867), William (b. 17 June 1869) and John (b. ~1872). Son William Smith was born on 17 June 1869 at Ordie, Logie Coldstone. William, a general carter, was dead by 1881 as his wife was a widow by then.

In 1881, Mary Smith, 45, a widow who *'knitts stockings &c'*, resided at No.4 Hamlet, Ordie, Logie Coldstone, with children Margaret, 14, and William, 11, both scholars, and John, 8. Mary Smith nee Simpson was dead by 1898.

Dave's paternal great-grandparents – William Barron and Helen Findlay

Dave's other paternal great-grandfather William Barron and his great-grandmother Helen Findlay were both born around 1830 in Aberdeenshire. William Barron, a mason journeyman, married Helen Findlay and they had two known daughters; Margaret (b. ~1868) and Helen Findlay Barron in Strathdon, Aberdeenshire. William, a mason journeyman, was dead by 1898, although, wife Helen was still alive at that time.

Dave's maternal great-grandparents – William Baigrie and Mary Wallace

Dave's maternal great-grandfather William Baigrie (or Bagrie) and great-grandmother Mary Wallace were both born around 1850 in Aberdeenshire. William Baigrie worked as a scavenger for the Aberdeen Corporation, an old term for the occupation of a bin man or refuse collector. The observant reader will have noted in Chapter 4 that John Greig was also descended from a Corporation scavenger ancestor in Edinburgh. William Baigrie, a scavenger, married wife Mary Wallace and they had two known children; Hugh Wallace (b. ~1879) and Isabella, aka Bella, in Aberdeenshire.

William, a scavenger, was dead by 1900, although, his wife Mary was still alive by then.

Dave's maternal great-grandparents – Alexander Burness and Margaret Collie

Dave's other maternal great-grandfather Alexander Burness was born around 1854 in Newhills, Aberdeenshire to father Alexander Burness, a gardener, and mother Margaret Cruikshank. The surname Burness was the more common spelling at that time in Aberdeenshire and Kincardineshire of the Lowland surname variant of Burns. The poet Robert Burns (1759-1796) was descended from his father William Burness (1721-1784) from Dunnottar, Kincardineshire, and the great bard Rabbie only stopped signing his name 'Burness' in 1786.

Dave's great-grandmother Margaret Collie, aka Maggie, was born around 1851 in Peterculter, Aberdeenshire to father Samuel Collie, a farm servant, and mother Jean Smith. Alexander Burness, 25, a farm servant, of Gillahills, Newhills, married Margaret Collie, 28, a domestic servant, of Hill of Cantlaw, Peterculter, on 28 February 1879. The wedding was conducted by Rev James Dalgarno, minister of Peterculter Free Church of Scotland; the witnesses were Samuel Collie and Sam Collie, Maggie's father and brother. Alexander, a marine stoker in Aberdeen, and Maggie had a daughter Margaret Cruikshank Burness (b. ~1880). Alexander, a marine stoker, and wife Maggie were still alive in 1900.

Dave's paternal great-great-grandparents –
William Smith and Margaret Smith

Dave's paternal great-great-grandfather William Smith and great-great-grandmother Margaret Smith were born around 1795 in Aberdeenshire. William Smith, a labourer, married Margaret Smith and they had two known sons; William (b. 9 December 1822) and Peter in Monellie, Forgue. Son William's birth is recorded in the OPRs for the parish of Forgue as follows:-

> *OPR Births Forgue 194/4/27*
>
> *1822: William lawful son of William Smith and Margaret Smith in Monellie was born 9th and baptized 15th December, Witnesses George Smith and James Alexander*

William, a labourer, was dead by 1866, although, wife Margaret was still alive by then.

Dave's paternal great-great-grandparents –
Robert Simpson and Ann Milne

His other paternal great-great-grandfather Robert Simpson and great-great-grandmother Ann Milne were both born around 1800 in Aboyne, Aberdeenshire. Robert Simpson, a farmer, married Ann Milne and they had a daughter Mary (b. ~1839) in Aboyne. Robert, a farmer, was dead by 1866, although, wife Ann was still alive by then.

Dave's maternal great-great-grandparents – Alexander Burness and Margaret Cruikshank

Dave's maternal great-great-grandfather Alexander Burness and great-great-grandmother Margaret Cruikshank were both born around 1825 in Aberdeenshire. Alexander Burness, a gardener, married Margaret Cruikshank and they had a son Alexander (b. ~1854) in Newhills. Alexander, a gardener, was dead by 1879, although, his wife Margaret was still alive by then.

Dave's maternal great-great-grandparents – Samuel Collie and Jean Smith

Dave's other maternal great-great-grandfather Samuel Collie and great-great-grandmother Jean Smith were both born around 1820 in Aberdeenshire. Samuel Collie, a farm servant, married Jean Smith and they had two known children in Peterculter; Samuel and Margaret, aka Maggie (b. ~1858). Samuel, a farm servant, and wife Jean were still alive in 1879 in Peterculter. Collie, meaning 'the black-haired one', is a common surname in the north-east of Scotland and the author's maternal grandmother was born Annie Caie Collie and her father Peter Beattie Collie was born illegitimately in Tarland, Aberdeenshire to mother Catherine Collie.

CHAPTER 7

Tommy McLean (outside right)

Honours as a Rangers player:
1 European Cup Winners' Cup
3 Scottish League titles
4 Scottish Cups
3 Scottish League Cups

The young Tommy McLean

Thomas McLean was born on 2 June 1947 in Ashgill, Dalserf, Lanarkshire, to father Thomas McLean, a baker, and mother Annie Smith Yuille. McLean's maternal grandfather William Yuille played professionally for Rangers before WWI. His father Tom had been a promising junior footballer before joining the Plymouth Brethren when he married Annie. Their three sons Willie, Jim and Tommy, who all went on to become professional footballers and managers, had a strict religious upbringing in the Brethern. McLean played as a midfielder and winger for Kilmarnock, Rangers and Scotland.

A traditional tricky winger, McLean started his career at Kilmarnock, where at one point all three brothers were at the club together, Jim and Tommy as players and Willie as a coach. In 1964-65, he was part of the Kilmarnock team which won the club's only Scottish League title. He joined Rangers in 1971 and was involved in the famous 1972 European Cup Winners' Cup triumph in Barcelona. He went on to play 452 times for Rangers, winning three Scottish League championships, four Scottish Cups and three Scottish League Cups. McLean was capped six times by Scotland, with all his appearances coming as a Kilmarnock player. He also represented the Scottish League seven times.

After his playing career ended he became Rangers' assistant manager. Later, he had spells in management with Morton, Motherwell, Hearts, Raith Rovers and Dundee United, before becoming Under-19 coach at Rangers. McLean managed Motherwell for ten years, during which the club won the Scottish Cup in 1991, defeating Dundee United, who were managed by his brother Jim.

Tommy's parents - Thomas McLean and Annie Smith Yuille

Tommy's father Thomas McLean was born on 7 January 1913 at 50 Raploch Street, Larkhall, to father William McLean, a coal miner, and mother Barbara Hamilton. When Tom left school he worked as a baker. He had also been a promising junior footballer with Larkhall Thistle, as recorded by his son Tommy, who wrote: *"My father's side were no strangers to the beautiful game either, with his brother William playing for Third Lanark. My dad was a force to be reckoned with in his own right in the juniors....most considered him to be the top McLean."*

Three months into WWI, the 'Battle of the Bees' was fought between British, Indian and German forces at Tanga, Tanzania on 4 November 1914. So-called because a huge beehive was disturbed during the battle and both offensive British and defensive Germans were attacked by bees. That same day, Tommy's mother Annie Smith Yuille was born on 4 November 1914 at Red Row, Dalserf, to father William Yuille, a coal miner, and mother Mary Marshall.

Thomas McLean, 21, a baker, of 44 Raploch Street, Larkhall, married Annie Smith Yuille, 19, a weaving factory hand, of 6 Douglas Drive, Ashgill, Dalserf, on 27 April 1934 in the Miner's Welfare Institute, Ashgill. The wedding was conducted by Pastor Robert Chapman of the Dalserf Christian Brethern; the best man was David Hamilton, Tom's cousin, and the best maid was Mary Gwynne Yuille, Annie's sister. Tom converted to the Christian Brethern and he and Annie brought their family up in the strict religious order. Tom and Annie had three sons in Larkhall; William, aka Willie, James Yuille, aka Jim (b. 2 August 1937) and Thomas, aka Tommy, (b. 2 June 1947). Although the boys were raised in the strict Plymouth Brethern sect they all went on to become successful professional footballers and managers.

Tommy's paternal grandparents - William McLean and Barbara Hamilton

Tommy's paternal grandfather William McLean was born on 18 June 1889 at 106 Meadowhill, Larkhall, to father Thomas

McLean, a coal miner, and mother Mary Brannan. Initially, William worked down the Lanarkshire coalfields but later became a railway surfaceman with the Caledonian Railway Company. Tommy's paternal grandmother Barbara Hamilton was born around 1894 in Glasgow to father David Hamilton, a coal miner, and mother Elizabeth Hamilton. Barbara, like many girls of the Victorian era, went into domestic service.

William McLean, 23, a coal miner, of 24 Marshall Street, Larkhall, married Barbara Hamilton, 18, a domestic servant, of 30 Young Street, Glasgow, on 28 June 1912 at 90½ Great Hamilton Street, Calton, Glasgow by warrant of the Sheriff Substitute of Lanarkshire in presence of John Pate, a van man, and Agnes Cook or Pate. Barbara was pregnant by William, which might explain the civil ceremony, and son Thomas McLean was born on 7 January 1913 at 50 Raploch Street, Larkhall. William and Barbara also had another son Willie who played for Third Lanark, whilst son Tom had a spell with Larkhall Thistle. William McLean, a railway surfaceman, was dead by 1934, however, his wife Barbara McLean nee Hamilton was still alive then.

Tommy's maternal grandparents - William Yuille and Mary Marshall

Tommy's maternal grandfather William Yuille was born around 1889 in Dalserf, Lanarkshire, to father James Yuille, a coal miner, and mother Annie Smith. Between 1908 and 1911 William Yuille played professionally with Rangers making his league debut on 12 December 1908 against

Hamilton Academicals. Grandson Tommy wrote: *"My mother's father, William Yuille, was a forward with Rangers and scored a few goals by all accounts."* William did not quite make the breakthrough at Rangers, playing only 16 first team games and scoring six times. William went back to coal mining and Tommy described him in the Scotsman as *'an auld bugger who was very strict'.*

Tommy's grandmother Mary Marshall was born around 1891, also in Dalserf, to father William Marshall and mother Mary Gwynne. William Yuille, 22, a coal miner, of Red Row, Dalserf, married Mary Marshall, 20, a domestic servant, of Tinto View, Dalserf, on 10 March 1911. The wedding was conducted by Rev Alexander Barclay BD, minister of Dalserf Parish Church; the best man was Robert Yuille, William's brother, and the best maid was Elizabeth Marshall, Mary's sister.

William and Mary had two known daughters; Annie Smith (b. 4 November 1914) and Mary Gwynne. Three months after the outbreak of WWI, daughter Annie Smith Yuille was born on 4 November 1914 at Red Row, Dalserf. William Yuille, a motor van man, was still alive in 1934, however, his wife Mary Yuille nee Marshall was dead by then.

Tommy's paternal great-grandparents -
Thomas McLean and Mary Brannan

Tommy's paternal great-grandfather Thomas McLean was born on 7 June 1864 in Cambusnethan, Lanarkshire, to father William McLean, a coal miner, and mother Jane McCombs. Tommy's great-grandmother Mary Brannan was born on 25

May 1860 in Shotts, Lanarkshire, to father James Brannan, a coal miner, and mother Catherine Higgins. William McLean, 19, a coal miner, married Mary Brannan, 19, a farm servant, both of Merryton Colliery Row, Hamilton on 10 January 1884 at County Buildings, Hamilton by warrant of the Sheriff Substitute for Lanarkshire in presence of Alexander McCormick, a miner, and Isabella Davidson McCormick.

The likelihood is this was a mixed marriage, which might explain the civil ceremony. Son William McLean was born on 18 June 1889 at 106 Meadowhill, Larkhall. Thomas McLean, a coal miner, was still alive in 1912, however, his wife Mary McLean nee Brannan was dead by then.

Tommy's paternal great-grandparents - David Hamilton and Elizabeth Hamilton

Tommy's other paternal great-grandfather David Hamilton and his great-grandmother Elizabeth Hamilton were both born around 1865 in Glasgow. David and Elizabeth had a daughter Barbara (b. ~1894) in Glasgow. David Hamilton, a coal miner, and his wife Elizabeth Hamilton nee Hamilton were both alive and living in Calton, Glasgow in 1912.

Tommy's maternal great-grandparents - James Yuille and Annie Smith

Tommy's maternal great-grandfather James Yuille and great-grandmother Annie Smith were both born around 1860 in Lanarkshire. James and Annie had two known sons in Dalserf;

William (b. ~1889) and Robert. James Yuille, a coal miner, and wife Annie Yuille nee Smith were both alive in 1911.

Tommy's maternal great-grandparents - William Marshall and Mary Gwynne

Tommy's other maternal great-grandfather William Marshall and great-grandmother Mary Gwynne were born around 1865 in Lanarkshire. William and Mary had two known daughters in Dalserf; Mary (b. ~1891) and Elizabeth. William Marshall, a coal miner, and wife Mary Marshall nee Gwynne were both still alive in 1911.

Tommy's paternal great-great-grandparents – William McLean and Jane McCombs

Tommy's paternal great-great-grandfather William McLean and great-great-grandmother Jane McCombs were born around 1835 in Lanarkshire. William McLean, a coal miner, married Jane McCombs on 31 December 1861 in Cambusnethan Parish Church and they had seven known children; in Cambusnethan, Sarah (b. 7 November 1862), Thomas (b. 16 June 1864), James (b. 31 March 1866), Margaret Docherty (b. 25 April 1868), William (b. 21 March 1870, died in infancy); and, in Dalserf, Janet (b. 29 March 1872) and another William (b. 18 April 1874). William McLean, a coal miner, and wife Jane McLean nee McCombs were both still alive in 1884.

Tommy's paternal great-great-grandparents – James Brannan and Catherine Higgins

Tommy's other paternal great-great-grandfather James Brannan and great-great-grandmother Catherine Higgins were born around 1835 in Ireland. James and Catherine, who were Roman Catholic, had two known daughters in Shotts, Lanarkshire; Bridget (b. 30 June 1857) and Mary (b. 25 May 1860). James Brannan, a coal miner, was dead by 1884, however, wife Catherine Brannan nee Higgins was still alive then.

CHAPTER 8

Alfie Conn (inside right)

Honours as a Rangers player:
1 European Cup Winners' Cup
1 Scottish Cup

The young Alfie Conn

Alfred James Conn was born on 5 April 1952 at 9 Grosvenor Street, Haymarket, Edinburgh to father Alfred Hotchkiss Conn, a professional footballer, and mother Elizabeth Baxter. At that time the family were living at 4 Ingliston Cottages, Newbridge, Edinburgh. Alfie's father, Alfie Conn senior, was also a professional footballer, having played for Heart of Midlothian and he was one of the 'Terrible Trio' at Tynecastle in the 1950s. Alfie Conn junior was controversially the first post-WWII player to sign for both Rangers and Celtic.

Conn made his senior debut for Rangers against Irish side Dundalk in the Fairs Cup tournament in November 1968. He was part of the Rangers team which lifted the European Cup Winners' Cup in 1972 and also helped the Ibrox team win the Scottish Cup in 1973, scoring their second goal in a 3-2 victory over Celtic at Hampden Park. He played for Tottenham Hotspur from 1974-77 and was the last player to be signed by Spurs manager Bill Nicholson. Despite playing only 35 games and scoring six goals, he was a huge fan favourite. He was dubbed the 'King of White Hart Lane', after scoring a hat-trick on his debut in a 5-2 win at Newcastle. In the final game of the 1974-75 season at White Hart Lane, Spurs had to beat Leeds United to prevent relegation from the First Division. Conn scored a goal, set up two others, and also cheekily sat on the ball, in a 4-2 victory. While at Spurs he made two appearances for the Scotland national team at the end of the season in 1975.

After leaving Spurs, Conn controversially signed for Celtic, in a period when the Troubles were at their height in Northern Ireland and the rivalry between the opposing fans at Ibrox and Parkhead had become intense. In 1977, Conn won another Scottish Cup medal with Celtic when they defeated Rangers 1-0 in the final, a feat that did not go down well with the Ibrox faithful. He then followed in his father's footsteps by signing for the Tynecastle club in 1980, after a short spell playing indoor football in the United States with Pittsburgh Spirit. After leaving Hearts, Conn ended his playing career with short spells at Blackpool and Motherwell before retiring in 1983.

Alfie's parents – Alfred Hotchkiss Conn and Elizabeth Baxter

Alfie's father Alfred Hotchkiss Conn was born on 2 October 1926 at 26 South Crescent, Prestonpans, East Lothian, to father James Conn, a stone miner, and mother Margaret Finlayson Goodfellow. His mother Elizabeth Baxter was born on 6 June 1931 at North Lodge, Preston Lodge, Prestonpans to father William Baxter, a coal miner hewer, and mother Margaret Edmond. Alfred Hotchkiss Conn, 24, a professional footballer, of 58 Preston Crescent, Prestonpans, married Elizabeth Baxter, 19, a live-in waitress at Ratho Golf Club, on 19 March 1951 at St Mary's Parish Church of Scotland, Ratho. The wedding was conducted by Rev Cyril Jones; the best man was James Conn, Alfie's brother, and the best maid was Margo Dunn. Son Alfred James Conn was born on 5 April 1952 at 9 Grosvenor Street, Haymarket, Edinburgh. At that time the family were living at 4 Ingliston Cottages, Newbridge, Edinburgh.

Like his son, Alfie Conn was also a professional footballer, famously part of the 'Terrible Trio' of the Heart of Midlothian side of the 1950s, along with Willie Bauld and Jimmy Wardhaugh. He joined Hearts from Inveresk Athletic in 1944, making his debut later that year in a 4-0 win over Dumbarton in a wartime Southern League match. He established himself in the first team in the 1948-49 season, when he combined with Bauld and Wardhaugh. Conn was an energetic, tenacious player with powerful shooting skills. In their first match as the Terrible Trio, the result was a 6-1 victory over East Fife. The Terrible Trio continued to score freely in the following five seasons, Conn notching 102 goals and Hearts became regular top four finishers.

Conn eventually won his first medal in the 1954-55 season, when Hearts defeated Motherwell 4-2 in the Scottish League Cup final. The following season, Conn scored as

Hearts defeated Celtic 3-1 in the 1956 Scottish Cup final, the Tynecastle team's first triumph in that competition for 50 years. He ended that 1955-56 season at the peak of his powers with a career-best 29 goals from 41 games. Two weeks after the cup win Conn attained his only Scotland cap on 2 May 1956 at Hampden Park, scoring after 12 minutes in a 1-1 draw with Austria. That year Conn suffered a serious ankle injury and would never be the same player again. In the league, he made only ten appearances in 1956-57 and only five for Hearts in 1957-58. He had scored 221 goals in 408 games for Hearts.

He transferred to Raith Rovers from 1958-60 and also had a short spell with Johannesburg Ramblers. Conn had a brief spell as manager of both Gala Fairydean and Raith Rovers. Conn watched his son, Alfie Conn junior, establish a successful footballing career of his own, notably seeing his son lift the 1972 ECWC with Rangers in Barcelona and also playing for Spurs, Celtic and his beloved Hearts. Alfred Hotchkiss Conn, 82, died on 7 January 2009.

Alfie's paternal grandparents – James Conn and Margaret Finlayson Goodfellow

Alfie's paternal grandfather James Conn was born on 28 February 1891 at 55 Ladywell Road, Dalziel, Motherwell to father Robert Conn, a hammerman, and mother Hannah Hotchkiss. Tragically, his mother Hannah died after James's birth at 7 am on the following morning of 1 March 1891. However, when Robert, still grieving, registered James's birth on 16 March 1891, he stated the mother was Sarah Ann Capewell (married name Hotchkiss), James's grandmother. James Conn was likely raised by his Hotchkiss grandparents and the registration of Sarah Ann may have indicated an informal adoption.

Alfie's paternal grandmother Margaret Finlayson Goodfellow, aka Maggie, was born around 1890 in Lanarkshire to father Peter Goodfellow, a mining contractor, and mother Jane Finlayson. Maggie was raised at Hougomont Place in the mining village of Waterloo, named in commemoration of the Lanarkshire regiments who defeated Napoleon Bonaparte. Château d'Hougoumont is a large farmhouse situated at the bottom of an escarpment near the Nivelles road in Braine-l'Alleud, near Waterloo, Belgium. The escarpment is where British and other allied forces faced Napoleon's army at the Battle of Waterloo on 18 June 1815.

James Conn, 21, a coal miner, of 147 Craigneuk Street, Wishaw, married Maggie Finlayson Goodfellow, 23, a sewing machinist, of Hougomont Place, Waterloo, on Hogmanay, 31 December 1913 at the Manse, Overtown. The wedding was conducted by Rev D L Thomson, minister of Overtown Church of Scotland; the best man was William Irvine and the best maid was Marion Goodfellow, Maggie's sister.

James, a coal miner and later a stone miner, and his wife Maggie had four known sons; Robert, Peter, James and Alfred. Son Robert Conn was born on 18 February 1915 at Hougomont Place, Waterloo. Son Peter Goodfellow Conn was born on 4 August 1916 at Hougomont Place, Waterloo. Son James Conn was born on 6 May 1923 at 15 Cambus Cottages, Newmains. Son Alfred Hotchkiss Conn was born on 2 October 1926 at 26 South Crescent, Prestonpans. James Conn, 73, a retired school janitor married to Margaret Goodfellow, of 6 Rope Walk, Prestonpans, died on his birthday, 28 February 1964, in the Royal Infirmary, Edinburgh of a massive pulmonary embolus and carcinoma of the stomach as certified by Dr Hans C Goldberg MB.

Alfie's maternal grandparents – William Baxter and Margaret Thomson Edmond

Alfie's maternal grandfather William Baxter was born around 1909 in Prestonpans, East Lothian to father William Baxter, a coal miner, and mother Susan Storrie. His grandmother Margaret Thomson Edmond was born around 1911 also in Prestonpans to father William Edmond, a coal miner, and mother Elizabeth Thomson. William Baxter, 21, a coal miner, of 16 Nimmo Avenue, Prestonpans, married Margaret Thomson Edmond, 19, a domestic servant, of Castlepark, Prestonpans, on 3 October 1930 at the Grange Manse, Prestonpans.

The marriage was a unique double wedding alongside Margaret's brother Charles Edmond, 27, a coal brusher, of Castlepark, who married Mary Ann Carroll, 19, a brewery worker, of 50 Middle Street, Cuthill, Prestonpans. The double wedding was conducted by Rev Kenneth MacLennan, minister of Grange Church of Scotland; the witnesses were Robert Storrie, William's cousin, Beatrice Blakey Edmond and James Edmond, respectively Margaret and Charles's sister and brother, and Lizzie Carroll, Mary Ann's sister.

Daughter Elizabeth Baxter was born on 6 June 1931 at North Lodge, Preston Lodge, Prestonpans to father William Baxter, a coal miner hewer, and mother Margaret Edmond. William, a miner, and Margaret were both still alive in 1951 in Prestonpans.

Alfie's paternal great-grandparents - Robert Conn and Hannah Hotchkiss

Alfie's paternal great-grandfather Robert Conn was born on 19 August 1862 at Chryston, Cadder, Lanarkshire to father Robert Conn, a forester, and mother Jane Greenlees. His grandmother Hannah Hotchkiss was born around 1864 in Cambusnethan, Lanarkshire to father William Hotchkiss, a blacksmith, and mother Sarah Ann Capewell. Robert Conn, 24, a gardener, of Muirhouse, Cambusnethan, married Hannah Hotchkiss, 23, of Excelsior Cottage, Shieldmuir, Motherwell, on 25 March 1887 at Motherwell Episcopal Church. The wedding was conducted by Fr M Fergus MA, priest curate in charge of Holy Trinity Mission Church; the best man was John Wotherspoon and the best maid was Agnes Hotchkiss, Hannah's sister.

Robert gave up the gardening trade to become a hammerman in the Lanarkshire ironworks at the nearby Excelsior Ironworks in Wishaw. Robert and Hannah had three known children; Robert (b. ~1888, Cambusnethan), Sarah Ann (b. ~1889, Cambusnethan) and James (b. 28 February 1891, Dalziel). Son James Conn was born on 28 February 1891 at 55 Ladywell Road, Dalziel, Motherwell, to father Robert

Conn, a hammerman, and mother Hannah Hotchkiss, although Robert registered his mother-in-law Sarah Ann Capewell. The reason for this apparent registration anomaly was because his wife Hannah died the morning after James's birth and his mother-in-law had informally adopted baby James. Hannah Conn nee Hotchkiss, only 27, married to Robert Conn, a hammerman, died on 1 March 1891 at 55 Ladywell Road, Dalziel, Motherwell of puerperal metritis, for 8 days, as certified by Dr James McDonald MB CM. Puerperal metritis is an acute systemic illness due to bacterial infection of the uterus.

Later in 1891, Robert Conn, 28, a widowed and unemployed gardener, boarded at 8 Newlands, Craigneuk, Dalziel, with children Robert, 3, and Sarah A, 2, at the home of English-born Charles Brotherton, 46, a blacksmith. It appears that baby James was being raised by his Hotchkiss grandparents. Robert Conn, 29, a widowed house gardener, of 26 Commonside, Airdrie, married second wife Janet, aka Jessie, Ewing nee Brown, 36, widow of Matthew Ewing, a coal miner, on 29 April 1892. The wedding was conducted by Rev John Cook, minister of Free High Church, Airdrie; the witnesses were John and E Laing.

Robert and Janet had three known children; Susan (b. ~1893, Irvine), Margaret (b. ~1896, Kirkintilloch) and Jane G (b. ~1900, Lennoxtown). Robert worked as a jobbing estate gardener and the family moved frequently around the West of Scotland seeking work. In 1901, Robert Conn, 38, a gardener domestic servant, resided at Ballochmount Cothouse, Maybole, with wife Janet, an outdoor worker, children Robert, 13, a scholar, Sarah Ann, 12, Susan, 8, Margaret,

5, and Jane G, 1. In the Ordnance Survey Name Books for 1855-57 Ballochmount was described as *'a thatched one storey cot house in middling repair, property of T H Crawford Esq.'* It can only be imagined what state of repair it was in 44 years later when Robert lived there. Robert Conn, a hammerman, was still alive in 1913.

Alfie's paternal great-grandparents - Peter Goodfellow and Jane Finlayson

Alfie's other paternal great-grandfather Peter Goodfellow and great-grandmother Jane Finlayson were both born around 1865 in Lanarkshire. Peter Goodfellow, a mining contractor, married Jane Finlayson and they had two known daughters; Marion and Margaret Finlayson (b. ~1890) in Lanarkshire. Peter, a mining contractor, and wife Jane were still alive in 1913 in Waterloo, Lanarkshire.

Alfie's maternal great-grandparents – William Baxter and Susan Storrie

Alfie's maternal great-grandfather William Baxter and great-grandmother Susan Storrie were both born around 1880 in Prestonpans. William Baxter, a coal miner, married Susan Storrie and they had a son William (b. ~1909) in Prestonpans. William, a coal miner, and Susan were still alive in 1930 in Prestonpans.

Alfie's maternal great-grandparents – William Edmond and Elizabeth Thomson

Alfie's other maternal great-grandfather William Edmond and great-grandmother Elizabeth Thomson were both born around 1880 in Prestonpans. William Edmond, a coal miner, married Elizabeth Thomson and they had two known daughters in Prestonpans; Margaret Thomson (b. ~1911) and Beatrice Blakey Edmond. William Edmond, a coal miner, was deceased by 1930 and his wife Elizabeth was still alive and had remarried a second husband surnamed Watson.

Alfie's paternal great-great-grandparents – Robert Conn and Jane Greenlees

Alfie's paternal great-great-grandfather Robert Conn and great-great-grandmother Jane Greenlees were both born about 1835 in Lanarkshire. Robert Conn, a forester, married Jane Greenlees and they had a son Robert (b. 19 August 1862) in Chryston, Cadder, Lanarkshire. Jane was dead by 1887, although, Robert, a gamekeeper, was still alive in 1892.

Alfie's paternal great-great-grandparents – William Hotchkiss and Sarah Ann Capewell

Alfie's other paternal great-great-grandfather William Hotchkiss and great-great-grandmother Sarah Ann Capewell were both born about 1835 in Lanarkshire. William Hotchkiss, a blacksmith, married Sarah Ann Capewell and they had two known daughters in Cambusnethan; Hannah (b. ~1864) and Agnes.

William got a job in the Excelsior Ironworks in Wishaw and he rose to be a foreman manager living with his family at Excelsior Cottage. The Excelsior Ironworks were established in the 1860s by Messrs J. Williams & Coy, pioneers of the iron nail industry in Scotland. The firm specialised in nails, staples, fencing wire and metal strips. William, a mechanical engineer's foreman, and Sarah Ann were still alive in March 1891 when their daughter Hannah died in childbirth and it appears that they adopted and raised their grandson James Conn, Alfie's grandfather.

CHAPTER 9

Colin Stein (centre forward)

Honours as a Rangers player:
1 European Cup Winners' Cup
2 Scottish League Cups

The young Colin Stein

Colin Anderson Stein was born on 10 May 1947 at 61 Hope Street, Philpstoun, Linlithgow, West Lothian, to father Robert Stein, an oil shale worker, and mother Helen Anderson. His elder brother, Bobby Stein, was also a professional footballer, who played for Broxburn Athletic, Raith Rovers and Montrose in the 1960s. Stein began his playing career with Armadale Thistle. He went on to play professionally for Hibernian, Rangers, Kilmarnock and the Scottish national team during the 1960s and 1970s. He also had a spell in England with Coventry City.

Stein was centre-forward on 26 November 1969 when the author's father Archie took him to Ibrox for the first time to see Rangers losing 3-1 to Gornik Zabrze in the return leg of the 1969-70 European Cup Winners' Cup. On 2 January

1971, during an Old Firm derby at Ibrox, Stein scored an equalising goal in stoppage time to salvage a draw for Rangers, after Celtic had taken the lead in the 89th minute. Minutes later, after full-time, barriers on Stairway 13 at Ibrox gave way, causing a chain-reaction pileup of spectators that killed 66 and injured over 200 in what would be commemorated as the 'Ibrox Disaster'. Initial reports speculated that Rangers supporters, who had left the ground early, turned back upon hearing the crowd roar at Stein's goal, causing the disaster. The official inquiry into the tragedy conclusively disproved this and concluded that all the spectators were moving away from the ground in the same direction at the time of the collapse.

Stein played a crucial part in Rangers winning the 1972 European Cup Winners' Cup, scoring the opening goal in the final. That season, Rangers beat Stade Rennes, Sporting CP, Torino, Bayern Munich and Dinamo Moscow to win the competition and Stein was one of only five players who played in every game of the campaign. After a spell with Coventry City, Stein returned to Rangers in 1975 and famously scored the equalising goal against his old team Hibernian to clinch the Scottish League Championship, denying Old Firm rivals Celtic the chance to win 10 in a row. Unfortunately, Stein had not played enough games that season to qualify for a championship medal.

In the twilight of his career, after leaving Kilmarnock, Stein played for Highland League side Elgin City. He also represented Scotland and the Scottish League XI. Stein scored nine goals in 21 appearances for Scotland, including four goals in a 1970 FIFA World Cup qualification match against Cyprus.

Colin's parents – Robert Scott Stein and Helen Scott Anderson

Colin's father Robert Scott Stein was born on 20 April 1901 at Philpstoun, Linlithgow, to father Alexander Stein, a shale miner, and mother Christina Paris. In 1911, Robert, 9, a scholar, resided at 11 The Avenue, Linlithgow, with his father Alex Stein, 47, a widowed shale miner, and his siblings. Robert Stein followed his father into the shale mining industry at the Philpstoun Oil Company in an era when shale rock was manually mined from underground and then the oil was extracted by processing the rock. The modern method is to extract shale oil by the controversial process of 'fracking', which at present has been banned in Scotland by the Scottish Government.

Colin's mother Helen Scott Anderson was born on 12 June 1906 at Summerhouse Cottage, Polmont, Stirlingshire, to father Colin Thompson Anderson, a mining inspector, and mother Mary McMeeking Ball. In 1911, Helen, 4, resided at Quakerfield, Bannockburn, St Ninian's, Stirling, with father Colin Anderson, 33, a coal miner hewer, mother Mary, 27, siblings Edith, 3, and John, 1. Helen Anderson became a domestic servant below stairs at 'The Binns House' in Abercorn.

The House of the Binns was originally a 15th-century three-storey manor house founded by James Meldrum of the Bynnis. Possibly standing on a Pictish site, the courtyard house was of east and west blocks, joined by a northern rectangular range, flanked by two low towers. Between 1612 and 1630, Thomas Dalyell absorbed the house to make a U-plan Renaissance mansion of two-and-a-half storeys and a garret, flanked by two northern stair turrets. In 1621, a Laigh Hall was created out of the original cellar in the main block. In the late 17th century, General Sir Tam Dalyell further extended the house, with more rooms being added in the mid-18th century. In 1812, the crow-stepped gables and pointed turrets were replaced by fashionable crenellations. It was the family home of Tam Dalyell, the Labour MP for West Lothian, who is renowned for the constitutional issue which was coined by Enoch Powell MP as *'the West Lothian Question'*. A mile north of the Binns House lies Blackness Castle.

Robert Scott Stein, 24, an oil shale miner, of 61 Hope Street, Philpstoun, Linlithgow, married Helen Scott Anderson, 25, a domestic servant, of The Binns House, Abercorn, on 16 December 1932 at nearby Blackness Castle, Carriden. The wedding was conducted by Rev Johnston Oliphant, minister at Abercorn Church of Scotland; the best man was D K Ball, of Blackness Castle, and Christina Paris Stein, of 25 Napier Road, Edinburgh, Robert's sister.

Son Colin Anderson Stein was born on 10 May 1947 at 61 Hope Street, Philpstoun, Linlithgow and they also had an older son Robert Stein. Both Colin and Bobby became professional footballers. Colin's parents Robert and Helen were both deceased by 1969 when Colin married his wife Linda in Linlithgow and they did not live to see their son's greatest footballing achievement in 1972 in Barcelona.

Colin's paternal grandparents – Alexander Stein and Christina Black Paris

Colin's paternal grandfather Alexander Stein, aka Alex, was born on 9 July 1863 at Mannerston, Abercorn, Linlithgowshire, to father William Stein, a ploughman, and mother Elizabeth Anthony. Mannerston Farm holdings, run by the fourth generation Faulds family, is now a farm shop, café and tearoom selling award-winning Mannerston's ice cream.

Colin's paternal grandmother Christina Black Paris was born around 1867 to father James Paris, a mines' oversman, and mother Elizabeth Emslie. Alexander Stein, 22, a shale miner, married Christina Black Paris, 18, both of Roseberry Terrace, East Breich, Livingstone, on New Year's Eve, 31 December 1886. The wedding was conducted by Rev James Wardrop, minister of the United Presbyterian Church; the best man was William Paris, Christina's brother, and the best maid was Ellen Stein, Alexander's sister.

Alexander and Christina had ten known children; James (b. ~1889, Livingstone), Alexander (b. ~1891, Kirkliston), John (b. ~1892, Kirkliston), David (b. ~1894, Kirkliston), George (b. ~1896, Kirkliston), Elizabeth, aka Lizzie (b. ~1900, Eccclesmachan), Robert Scott (b. 20 April 1901, Philpstoun), Peter (b. ~1903, Linlithgow), Henry (b. ~1905, Linlithgow) and Christina Paris (b. ~1906, Linlithgow). Christina Stein nee Paris, only 38, died on 20 December 1907 at Bridgend, Linlithgow of a haemorrhage due to the rupture of uterine vessels as certified by Dr R B Thom MB ChB.

In 1911, Alex Stein, 47, a widowed shale miner, resided at 11 The Avenue, Linlithgow, with his children James, 22,

Alex, 20, and John, 19, all miner's drawers, David, 17, an underground pony driver, George, 15, also a miner's drawer, and Lizzie, 11, Robert, 9, Peter, 8, Henry, 6, and Christina, 5, all at school. Also residing with Alex were his two unmarried sisters-in-law Elizabeth Paris, 33, a housekeeper, and Mary Paris, 20, a general domestic servant.

On 18 February 1918, in the last year of WWI, the German army launched its final offensive on the Eastern Front against the Russian Red Guard codenamed 'Operation Faustschlag' meaning 'fist punch'. That same day Alexander Stein, only 53, a shale miner, died at Kinnaird Terrace, Philpstoun, Linlithgow, of cardiac weakness as certified by Dr Robert Cross MB CM. Alexander and Christina's son Alexander was also a shale miner for the Philpstoun Oil Works in Linlithgow as recorded on the Valuation Roll of West Lothian for 1935-36:-

> *Valuation Roll of the County of West Lothian for the Year 1935-36 – Parish of Linlithgow: 719: House 6 Hope Street, Wester Pardovan: [Proprietor] Ross James & Co. Philpstoun Oil Works Limited, 53 Bothwell Street, Glasgow: [Tenant] Alexander Stein, miner: [Annual Rent] £8 12s 7d*

Colin's maternal grandparents – Colin Thomson Anderson and Mary McMeeking Ball

Colin Anderson Stein was named after his maternal grandfather. Colin Thomson Anderson was born on 16 July 1877 at Baileyside, Falkirk, Stirlingshire to father John Anderson, a coal miner, and mother Agnes Thomson. Colin's maternal grandmother Mary McMeeking Ball was born on 25 November 1872 in Kirkcudbright in the Stewartry of Kirkcudbright to father John Ball, a tailor, and mother Helen Scott.

Colin Thomson Anderson, 25, an inspector of mines, of Shieldhill, Falkirk, married Mary McMeeking Ball, 25, a dressmaker, of Atkinson Place, Kirkcudbright, on 10 July 1903. The wedding was conducted by Rev A D Campbell, minister of Kirkcudbright Church of Scotland; the best man was John Anderson, Colin's brother, and the best maid was Robina Laurie. Colin and Mary had three known children in Polmont, Stirlingshire; Helen Scott (b. 12 June 1906), Edith (b. ~1908) and John (b. ~1910). In 1911, Colin Anderson, 33, a coal miner hewer, resided at Quakerfield, Bannockburn, St Ninian's, Stirling, with wife Mary, 27, children Helen, 4, Edith, 3, and John, 1. Colin, a mines inspector, and Mary were still alive in 1932.

Colin's paternal great-grandparents – William Stein and Elizabeth Anthony

Colin's paternal great-grandfather William Stein was born around 1820 in Linlithgow to father William Stein, a farm servant, and his great-grandmother Elizabeth Anthony was born around 1820 in Ratho, Midlothian to father David Anthony, a farm servant. It can be read in Chapter 8 that Alfie Conn also had family connections to Ratho. William Stein, a ploughman, married Elizabeth Anthony on 10 June 1842 at the Manse, Linlithgow, and the marriage was proclaimed, as was customary, in their respective parishes of Linlithgow and Muiravonside, Stirlingshire.

> *OPR Marriages Linlithgow 668/12/372*
>
> *1842: Stein: William: Ploughman: [residing] Muiravonside: [born] Linlithgow: [Father] W[illia]m Stein: Farm Servant*
>
> *1842: Anthony: Elisabeth: ~ : [residing] Linlithgow: [born] Ratho: [Father] David Anthony: Farm Servant: [when proclaimed] 22nd, 29th May & 5th June*
>
> *OPR Marriages Muiravonside 486/2/126*
>
> *1842: William Stein a parishioner & Elisabeth Anthony Linlithgow parish: [proclaimed] May 20: [married] June 10th*

William and Elizabeth had two known children; Ellen and Alexander (b. 9 June 1863). William and Elizabeth were both dead by 1887.

Colin's paternal great-grandparents – James Paris and Elizabeth Emslie

Colin's other paternal great-grandfather James Paris and great-grandmother Elizabeth Emslie were both born about 1840 in Linlithgowshire. James and Elizabeth had four known children; William, Christina Black (b. ~1867), Elizabeth (b. ~1878) and Mary (b. ~1891). James, a mines' overseer, and Elizabeth were both still alive in 1891 and residing at East Breich, Livingstone.

Colin's maternal great-grandparents – John Anderson and Agnes Thomson

Colin's maternal great-grandfather John Anderson and great-grandmother Agnes Thomson were both born around 1850 in Stirlingshire. John Anderson, a coal miner, married Agnes Thomson and they had two known sons; John and Colin Thomson (b. 16 July 1877) in Falkirk. John, a mines' oversman, and Agnes were still alive in 1903 and residing in Falkirk.

Colin's maternal great-grandparents – John Baul and Helen Scott or Swords

Colin's other maternal great-grandfather John Baul (or Ball) was born around 1840 in Wigtownshire to father Joseph Baul, a labourer, and mother Mary Kelly. His great-grandmother Helen Scott, or Swords, was born illegitimately around 1842 in Wigtownshire to father William Swords, a scourer in a woollen mill, and mother Margaret Scott. John Baul, 20, a tailor journeyman, of Newton Stewart, married Helen Scott or Swords, 18, who signed with her 'x' mark, of Kirkcowan, Wigtownshire, on 31 July 1860. The wedding was conducted by Rev James Charles, minister of Kirkcowan Church of Scotland; the witnesses were William Swords, Helen's father, and David Crozier. John and Helen had a daughter Mary McMeeking (b. 25 November 1872) in Kirkcudbright. John, a tailor, and Helen were both still alive in 1903.

Colin's paternal great-great-grandfathers –
William Stein and David Anthony

Colin's paternal great-great-grandfathers William Stein and David Anthony were both born about 1795. William Stein had a son William (b. ~1820) in Linlithgow and David Anthony had a daughter Elizabeth (b. ~1820) in Ratho, Edinburghshire, now called Midlothian.

Colin's maternal great-great-grandparents –
Joseph Baul and Mary Kelly

Colin's maternal great-great-grandfather Joseph Baul (or Ball) and great-great-grandmother Mary Kelly were born around 1810 in Wigtownshire. Joseph Baul, a labourer, married Mary Kelly and they had a son John (b. ~1840). Joseph and Mary were still alive in 1860 residing in Newton Stewart, Wigtownshire.

Colin's maternal great-great-grandparents –
William Swords and Margaret Scott

Colin's other maternal great-great-grandfather William Swords (or Sword or Seward) and great-great-grandmother Margaret Scott were both born around 1810 in Wigtownshire. William Swords, a scourer in a woollen mill, met Margaret Scott and they had an illegitimate daughter Helen Scott or Swords (b. ~1842). William and Margaret were still alive in 1860 residing in Kirkcowan, Wigtownshire.

CHAPTER 10

Alex MacDonald (inside left)

Honours as a Rangers player:
1 European Cup Winners' Cup
3 Scottish League titles
4 Scottish Cups
4 Scottish League Cups

The young Alex MacDonald

Named after his Hebridean grandfather, Alexander MacDonald was born on 17 March 1948 at 44 Gloucester Street, Tradeston, Glasgow, about a mile from his beloved Ibrox Stadium, to father John MacDonald, a plumber's labourer, and mother Agnes Watson. In the late 1950s, Alex's family moved from Tradeston to the new housing scheme of Easterhouse in the east end of Glasgow. After being bullied there on the football pitches, Alex, with his parents' consent, *"moved back to stay with his Granny Watson in Govanhill"*. This allowed him to continue his schooling on the south-side at Crookston Primary and Secondary Schools. Alex also spoke fondly of his other grandmother: *"Granny MacDonald and I were close as well. She came to Glasgow from*

*Uist and spoke the Gaelic. Hers was the Catholic side of the family.
But my da wasn't much into religion, so he didn't press it on me."*
In his youth, MacDonald was a big Rangers fan and his hero
was Jim Baxter.

MacDonald is a former professional football player and
manager. He played for St Johnstone, Rangers and Hearts
and also played in one full international match for Scotland
in 1976. MacDonald started his career with St Johnstone but
was signed by Rangers' manager Davie White in November
1968 for £65,000. He quickly became a fans favourite at Ibrox
and he was instrumental in Rangers 1972 Cup Winners' Cup
triumph, scoring against Stade Rennes in the first round.
During his time at Rangers, he played 503 games and scored
94 times and won medals in three Scottish League titles, four
Scottish Cups and four Scottish League Cups.

Towards the end of his playing career, MacDonald joined
Hearts for £30,000 in 1980 as player-manager. He led the
team as they won promotion in 1983, then narrowly missed
out on winning the Scottish League championship in 1986,
taking Hearts famously to within seven minutes of lifting the
title. MacDonald then managed Airdrieonians for most of
the 1990s, leading the team to Scottish Cup finals in 1992
and 1995.

Alex's parents – John MacDonald and Agnes Watson

Alex's father John MacDonald was born on 31 May 1922
at 195 Crookston Street, Gorbals, Glasgow, to father
Alexander MacDonald, an iron foundry labourer, and

mother Annie Shannon. It seems likely John was raised as a Roman Catholic, although he converted when he married. Alex's mother Agnes Watson was born on 11 June 1925 at 50 Commerce Street, Tradeston, Glasgow, to father Robert Watson, a carter, and mother Margaret Carlin.

John MacDonald, 25, a plumber's labourer, of 27 Paterson Street, Kingston, Glasgow, married Agnes Watson, 22, a sewing machinist, of 44 Gloucester Street, Tradeston, Glasgow, on 15 August 1947 at 137 Titwood Road, Strathbungo, Glasgow. The wedding was conducted by Rev John MacKay, minister of Gorbals-John Knox Church of Scotland; the best man was Donald MacDonald, John's brother, and the best maid was Janet C Watson, Agnes's sister. Son Alexander MacDonald was born on 17 March 1948 at 44 Gloucester Street, Tradeston, Glasgow. In the late 1950s, the MacDonald family moved to the new housing scheme of Easterhouse in the east end of Glasgow, however, after being continually bullied on the football pitches, their son Alex moved back to live with his Granny Watson in Govanhill.

Alex's paternal grandparents – Alexander MacDonald and Annie Shannon

Alex's paternal grandfather Alexander MacDonald, aka Alex, was born on 13 December 1885 at Garrynamonie, Lochboisdale, South Uist to father Angus MacDonald, a crofter, and mother Ann MacDonald. In 1901, Alexander, 15, a crofter's son, who spoke Gaelic and English, resided at the crofter's house in Garrynamonie, Lochboisdale, with his Gaelic speaking father Angus MacDonald, 72, a crofter, mother Ann, 60, brother Donald, 21, a crofter's son, and sister Effie, 18, a crofter's daughter.

South Uist, the second largest island in the Outer Hebrides, remains predominantly a Roman Catholic population. Legend had it that a Protestant minister was sent by the Presbytery to convert the island but he turned his little boat back during a fierce storm. In 1722, just a few miles north of Garrynamonie at Milton, Lochboisdale, the famous Flora MacDonald was born on South Uist. Following the Jacobite defeat at Culloden in 1746 and along with her cousin Neil MacEachen of Howbeg, they initially hid Bonnie Prince Charlie in a cave on South Uist. They then dressed the prince in woman's clothing and 'rowed him o'er the sea to Skye', where a French ship took Charlie and MacEachen to exile in France.

As the French could not pronounce his surname, Neil MacEachen changed to his mother's surname of MacDonald, Flora's aunt. His son became Marshal Etienne Jacques Joseph Alexandre MacDonald, 1st Duke of Taranto (1765-1840), one of Napoleon Bonaparte's most trusted and loyal generals. However, in 1814, when Napoleon was incarcerated in St Helena and the Bourbon dynasty was restored, MacDonald pledged allegiance to the restored monarchy. He refused to back Napoleon during the Hundred Days War and he was not on the battlefield at the Emperor's final defeat at Waterloo in 1815. In 1825, Marshal MacDonald famously made a trip to South Uist to visit 'Charlie's cave' and the lowly family croft at Howbeg. The whole island turned out to greet him as a returning hero. The islanders all claimed to be related to the great Marshal and they probably were not far wrong, as intermarriage was prevalent on the strictly Catholic island.

Alex's paternal grandmother Annie Shannon, aka Ann, was born around 1888 at Smerclate, South Uist to father Thomas Shannon, a farm labourer, and mother Christina Campbell. Her father Thomas was dead by 1891 and it appears that Annie was being raised by her widowed grandmother Ann Campbell. In 1891, Gaelic-speaking Ann Shannon, 3, resided at 39 Smerclate, South Uist, with her grandmother Ann Campbell, 65, a widowed crofter, her aunt Marion, 29, a general domestic servant, her uncle Donald, 27, a croft labourer, and her aunt Ann, 26, an agricultural servant. In 1901, Annie Shannon, 13, a scholar with Gaelic and English, resided at the crofter's house in Smerclate, with her uncle Donald Campbell, 40, a crofter, and her aunt Marion Docherty, 42, a widowed crofter's sister.

Alex MacDonald, 27, an iron foundry labourer, of 2 Thomson Terrace, Moorpark, Renfrew, married Annie Shannon, 16, a domestic servant, of 19 Newry Street, Scotstoun, on New Year's Day, 1 January 1915, during WWI, at the Church of the Holy Redeemer, Clydebank. The wedding was conducted by Fr Charles E Fleming, Roman Catholic priest; the best man was Daniel Wallace and the best maid was Kate Morrison.

Alex and Annie had three known sons; Angus, Donald and John. Son John MacDonald was born on 31 May 1922 at 195 Crookston Street, Gorbals, Glasgow. Alexander MacDonald, only 52, a foundry labourer, died on 23 January 1938 at 27 Paterson Street, Kingston, Glasgow of myocardial degeneration and hyperthyroidism as registered by his son Angus MacDonald. Annie MacDonald nee Shannon, 73, still residing at 27 Paterson Street, Kingston, Glasgow, died on 5 June 1961 at the Southern General Hospital of bronchopneumonia and ischaemic heart disease.

Alex's maternal grandparents – Robert Watson and Margaret Brown Carlin

Alex's maternal grandfather Robert Watson was born around 1901 in Glasgow to father Adam Watson, an engine fitter, and mother Margaret O'Neil. His grandmother Margaret Brown Carlin, aka Maggie, was born around 1903 in Glasgow to father Thomas Carlin, a carter, and mother Margaret Brown. Robert Watson, 21, of 31 Dale Street, Gorbals, Glasgow, married Margaret Brown Carlin, 19, an oatcake baker, of 155 Centre Street, Gorbals, Glasgow, on 7 July 1922 at the Gospel Mission Church, 198 Wallace Street, Glasgow. The wedding was conducted by Pastor Thomas Todd; the best man was John Cryans and the best maid was Agnes Cryans.

In the 1920s and 1930s, the Gorbals district was fast becoming the most deprived and overcrowded slum area in Glasgow. The Gorbals earned Glasgow its unflattering moniker of 'No Mean City' in the pre-WWII era of the Great Depression. Daughter Agnes Watson was born on 11 June 1925 at 50 Commerce Street, Tradeston, Glasgow. Robert Watson, a baths attendant, was dead by 1947, although, wife Margaret was still alive by then. In the late 1950s, Alex MacDonald moved back from Easterhouse to stay with his "Granny Watson" and continue his schooling on the south-side.

Alex's paternal great-grandparents – Angus MacDonald and Ann MacDonald

Alex's paternal great-grandfather Angus MacDonald (or McDonald) was born around 1841 in Lochboisdale, South Uist to father Donald MacDonald, a farmer, and mother Margaret Walker. His great-grandmother Ann MacDonald, aka Annie, was born around 1848 in Lochboisdale, South Uist to father Angus MacDonald, a farmer, and mother Catherine McLellan. Angus MacDonald, 30, a farmer, who signed with his 'x' mark, married wife Ann MacDonald, 23, who signed with her 'x' mark, both of Garrynamonie, Lochboisdale, on 17 January 1871. The wedding was conducted by Fr Donald MacColl, Roman Catholic clergyman; the witnesses were Archibald McLellan, Catherine's cousin, and Donald MacIntyre.

Father Donald MacColl was born in 1835 at Ardgour, Argyllshire and he preached at the South Uist chapels at Iochdar (1862-67); Bornish (1867-74) and Iochdar (1877-1887), during a period of great social upheaval and deprivation suffered by the islanders on South Uist, under the auspices of the influential Bishop Angus MacDonald. In the period of MacColl's tenure as the parish priest, many of the MacDonald clan of Garrynamonie and all across South Uist emigrated to the increasingly industrialised Central Belt of Scotland and many went over to Canada.

Angus and Ann had four known children in South Uist; Angus, Donald (b. ~1880), Euphemia aka Effie (b. ~1883) and Alexander (b. 13 December 1885). Son Alexander MacDonald, aka Alex, was born on 13 December 1885 at Garrynamonie, Lochboisdale, South Uist. In 1901, Gaelic speaking Angus MacDonald, 72, a crofter, resided at his crofter's house in Garrynamonie, Lochboisdale, with his wife Ann, 60, children Donald, 21, a crofter's son, Effie, 18, a crofter's daughter, Alexander, 15, a crofter's son, and grandson Angus Auld, 3.

Angus MacDonald, stated as 72, a crofter, married to Ann MacDonald, died on 23 January 1907 at Garrynamonie, Lochboisdale of an enlarged prostate, urine retention and old age as certified by Dr L McDonald LRCP. The death was registered by his son Angus MacDonald at Boisdale. Ann MacDonald nee MacDonald stated as 84, died on 19 February 1928 at Garrynamonie, Lochboisdale of senile decay as registered by her son Angus at Boisdale.

Alex's paternal great-grandparents – Thomas Shannon and Christina Campbell

Alex's other paternal great-grandfather Thomas Shannon and great-grandmother Christina Campbell, aka Christian, were both born around 1855 on South Uist, Inverness-shire. Christina's mother was Ann Campbell (her married name). Thomas Shannon, a farm labourer, married Christina Campbell and they had a daughter Annie (b. ~1888) at Smerclate, South Uist. Thomas Shannon, a farm labourer, was dead by 1891. Christina Shannon nee Campbell was still alive in 1915, although, she was dead by 1938.

Alex's maternal great-grandparents – Adam Watson and Margaret O'Neil

Alex's maternal great-grandfather Adam Watson and great-grandmother Margaret O'Neil were both born around 1875 in Glasgow. Adam Watson, an engine fitter, married Margaret O'Neil and they had a son Robert (b. ~1901) in Glasgow. Adam, an engine fitter, and wife Margaret were both still alive in 1922 in the slum-ridden Gorbals district of Glasgow.

Alex's maternal great-grandparents – Thomas Carlin and Margaret Brown

Alex's other maternal great-grandfather Thomas Carlin and great-grandmother Margaret Brown were both born around 1875 in Glasgow. Thomas Carlin, a carter, married Margaret Brown and they had a daughter Margaret Brown Carlin (b. ~1903) in Glasgow. Thomas, a carter, and wife Margaret were both still alive in 1922 also in the Gorbals district of Glasgow.

Alex's paternal great-great-grandparents – Donald MacDonald and Margaret Walker

Alex's paternal great-great-grandfather Donald MacDonald

and great-great-grandmother Margaret Walker were both born around 1815 in Lochboisdale, South Uist. Donald MacDonald, a farmer, married Margaret Walker and they had a son Angus (b. ~1841) in Lochboisdale. Donald MacDonald, a farmer, was dead by 1871. Margaret MacDonald nee Walker was still alive by then, although, she was dead by 1907.

Alex's paternal great-great-grandparents – Angus MacDonald and Catherine McLellan

Alex's other paternal great-great-grandfather Angus MacDonald and great-great-grandmother Catherine McLellan were both born around 1820 in Lochboisdale, South Uist. Angus MacDonald, a farmer, married Catherine McLellan and they had a daughter Ann aka Annie (b. ~1848) in Lochboisdale. Angus, a farmer, was still alive in 1871, although, wife Catherine was dead by then. Angus MacDonald, a crofter, was dead before 1928.

Alex's paternal great-great-grandmother – Ann Campbell (her married name)

Alex's other paternal great-great-grandmother Ann Campbell (her married name) was born around 1826 in South Uist, Inverness-shire. Ann married a husband surnamed Campbell and they had four known children in South Uist; Christian aka Christina (b. ~1855), Marion (b. ~1862), Donald (b. ~1864) and Ann (b. ~1865). In 1891, Gaelic-speaking Ann

Campbell, 65, a widowed crofter, resided at 39 Smerclate, South Uist, with children Marion, 29, a general domestic servant, Donald, 27, a croft labourer, and Ann, 26, an agricultural servant. Also living there were her two grandchildren; Marion's daughter Sarah Docherty, 8, a scholar, and Christina's daughter Ann Shannon, 3. Ann Campbell of Smerclate, South Uist was dead by 1901.

CHAPTER 11

Willie Johnston (outside left)

Honours as a Rangers player:
1 European Cup Winners' Cup
2 Scottish Cups
2 Scottish League Cups

The young Willie Johnston

William McClure Johnston was born on 19 December 1946 at 9 Shannon Street, Maryhill, Glasgow, to father William Copland Johnston, a tobacconist's assistant, and mother Catherine McClure. Although he was born in the city where he made his name as a footballer, Johnston was raised in Cardenden, Fife and like his father, he worked as a miner after leaving school. He is a former professional footballer, best remembered for his time at Rangers and West Bromwich Albion, although he had short spells at Hearts and Vancouver Whitecaps. Willie was known by the nickname 'Bud'. He began his career at local junior club Lochore Welfare when he signed schoolboy forms with Rangers. He joined the Gers full-time in 1964, aged 17, and made his debut against St Johnstone in the Scottish League Cup on 29 August 1964.

Two months later, following an injury to the established outside left Davie Wilson, Johnston was named in the side for the Scottish League Cup final and received his first winner's medal after a 2-1 Old Firm victory over Celtic. Johnston played in the outside left position on that cold, damp evening on 26 November 1969, when the author went with his father Archie to Ibrox and watched the Gers knocked out 2-6 on aggregate by Polish side Gornik Zabrze.

Johnston famously scored twice in the final as Rangers won the European Cup-Winners' Cup in 1972 by defeating Dinamo Moscow 3-2 in Barcelona. By that time he was often playing as a striker alongside Colin Stein, who scored Rangers opening goal in the final, as formations were modified. In December 1972 Johnston moved to England to join West Bromwich Albion, making his debut against Liverpool in the same month. Albion had paid a club record of £138,000 to bring him to The Hawthorns. He made 22 international appearances for Scotland and was selected for the 1978 FIFA World Cup squad in Argentina. However, he was controversially sent home by manager Ally MacLeod from Scotland's disastrous tournament after failing a drugs test. Johnston returned to Rangers in 1980 to play under former teammate John Greig, picking up a second Scottish Cup medal in 1981.

Willie's parents – William Copland Johnston and Catherine McClure

Willie's father William Copland Johnston represents a complex story of illegitimacy. He was registered as William Johnstone Anderson or Copland on 4 February 1918, in the final year of WWI, at 5 Panmure Place, St Giles, Edinburgh, to mother Marion Anderson, widow of William Copland, a Singer sewing machine factory worker, who had died on 16 August 1909 in Clydebank, Dunbartonshire. Marion Copland registered the birth but she did not name a father. However, William later stated his 'father of repute' was William Johnston, a coal miner, and his name was changed to William Copland Johnston.

Willie's mother Catherine McClure was born on 13 December 1924 at 7 Union Place, Anderston, Glasgow, to father George McClure, a hoist attendant, and mother Rosina Costley. After leaving school William Copland Johnston worked as a coal miner, however, at the outbreak of WWII, he enlisted in the Royal Army Ordnance Corps rising to the rank of Company Sergeant Major. William Copland Johnston, 27, a Company Sergeant Major RAOC, now engaged in War Service, married Catherine McClure, 20, of 9 Shannon Street, Maryhill, Glasgow, on 28 July 1945 in the Blythswood Registry Office.

By that time the war in Europe had ended on V E Day on 8 May 1945 but the War in Japan rumbled on for another 5 weeks after the wedding. Japanese Emperor Hirohito finally surrendered on 2 September 1945 following extended carpet bombing of Japanese cities, including the US Air Force dropping devastating atomic bombs on Hiroshima and Nagasaki and the Soviet Union invasion of the Korean Peninsula.

The following year son William McClure Johnston was born on 19 December 1946 at 9 Shannon Street, Maryhill, Glasgow, to father William Copland Johnston, a tobacconist's assistant, and mother Catherine McClure. The family moved through to Cardenden in Fife and William took a job as a coal miner in the Fife coalfields. They lived at 139 Carden Castle Park, Cardenden, however, William was back through in Glasgow in 1964 when he was killed in a tragic accident.

William Copland Johnston (formerly William Johnstone Copland), only 46, a coal miner, married to Catherine McClure, died on 2 March 1964 on Springburn Road, Glasgow of multiple injuries as seen after death by Dr J A Imrie MD. In a Register of Corrected Entries, it was recorded that William died on *'2nd March 1964 about 10h 5m PM in Springburn Road, Glasgow near Petershill Road in an ambulance between there and the Royal Infirmary of multiple injuries'*. The death was registered by his young 17-year-old son William, of 139 Carden Castle Park, Cardenden, who was just on the cusp of the breakthrough into the Rangers team that his father did not live to see.

Willie's paternal grandparents – William Johnston and Marion Anderson

Willie's paternal 'grandfather of repute' was known as William Johnston (or Johnstone) born around 1885, although little is known about him. Willie's paternal grandmother Marion

Anderson, aka Minnie, was born on 10 February 1885 at 1 Union Street, Clydebank, Dunbartonshire, to father John Anderson, a joiner journeyman, and mother Isabella Gordon Ritchie. Marion Anderson, 20, a dairymaid, of 1 Union Street, Clydebank, married husband William Copland, 24, a needle maker at the world-renowned Singer's Sewing Machines, of 150 Kilbowie Road, Clydebank, on 5 January 1905. The wedding was conducted by Rev George W Taylor of the United Free Church; the best man was Alexander Fraser and the best maid was Lilias Anderson, Marion's sister.

William and Marion had three known daughters; Isabella (b. ~1905, Scotstoun), Mary (b. ~1907, Clydebank) and Elizabeth (b. ~1909, Clydebank). However, William Copland died on 16 August 1909. In 1911, Marion A Copland, 26, a widow, and her three daughters Isabella, 6, Mary, 4 and Elizabeth, 2, resided at 4 Roseberry Place, Clydebank, with her father John Anderson, 61, a joiner in the John Brown & Coy shipyards, her mother Isabella, 57, and her other siblings.

It was in 1917, during WWI, that Marion met William Johnston (or Johnstone), a coal miner, and she fell pregnant. Son William Johnstone Anderson or Copland was born on 4 February 1918 at 5 Panmure Place, St Giles, Edinburgh, to mother Marion Anderson, widow of William Copland, a Singer sewing machine factory worker, 'who died on 16 August 1909' in Clydebank. It is possible that William Johnston, a coal miner, married Marion Copland or Anderson after the end of WWI. William and Marion were both dead by 1945.

Willie's maternal grandparents – George McClure and Rosina Costley

Willie's maternal grandfather George McClure was born around 1900 in Anderston, Glasgow to father Valentine McClure, a hammerman, and mother Mary Jane Garrity. In 1901, George, 1, resided at Back Land, 75 Brown Street, Broomielaw, Glasgow, with his father Valentine McClure, 25, a blacksmith's hammerman, mother Mary Jane, 25, a shirt machinist, and sister Helen, 3.

Willie's grandmother Rosina Costley was born around 1903 in Anderston, Glasgow to father William Costley, an engine keeper, and mother Catherine Rankin. George McClure, 22, a hoist attendant, of 9 Richard Street, Anderston, married Rosina Costley, 19, a pudding maker, of 8 Bishop Street, Anderston, on 28 April 1922 at 5 India Street, Glasgow. The wedding was conducted by Rev M Lamont, minister of St Mark's Church of Scotland; the best man was William Smith and the best maid was Essie Johnston. Daughter Catherine McClure was born on 13 December 1924 at 7 Union Place, Anderston, Glasgow, to father George McClure, a hoist attendant, and mother Rosina Costley. George McClure, a rubber work gateman, and wife Rosina were both still alive in 1945 in Glasgow.

Willie's paternal great-grandparents – John Anderson and Isabella Gordon Ritchie

Willie's paternal great-grandfather John Anderson was born around 1850 in North Leith, Edinburgh to father James Anderson, a ship carpenter journeyman, and mother Agnes

Aitken. His grandmother Isabella Gordon Ritchie was born around 1854 in Dirleton, Haddingtonshire to father David Ritchie, a master shoemaker, and mother Marion Crawford.

John Anderson, 25, a joiner journeyman, of 4 Bellgrove Street, Dennistoun, Glasgow, married Isabella Gordon Ritchie, 21, a teacher, of 17 King Street, South Leith, on 16 July 1875 at Wellpark Church of Scotland, Glasgow. The wedding was conducted by Rev Robert Thomson; the witnesses were William Thomson Exelby and Mary Ann Dowson Exelby. John and Isabella then moved to Clydebank, Dunbartonshire and then John was employed as a joiner journeyman in the Clydebank shipbuilding industry, at the world-renowned John Brown & Coy, famed for building state of the art warships and passenger liners, such as the Queen Mary, Queen Elizabeth and the QE2.

John and Isabella had 11 children in Clydebank, although two children died in infancy. They included Marion aka Minnie (b. 10 February 1885), Lilias (b. ~1887), Elizabeth (b. ~1889), Mary (b. ~1891), Christina (b. ~1894) and John (b. ~1899). Daughter Marion Anderson was born on 10 February 1885 at 1 Union Street, Clydebank. In 1911, John Anderson, 61, a joiner in the shipbuilding industry, resided at 4 Roseberry Place, Clydebank, with wife Isabella, 57, children Lilias, 24, a machinist in the Singer Sewing Machine factory, Elizabeth, 22, a student teacher, Mary, 20, a grocer's shop assistant, Christina, 17, a tracer at John Brown's shipyards, and John, 12. Also living at John's home was his widowed daughter Marion A Copland, 26, and her three daughters Isabella, 6, Mary, 4 and Elizabeth, 2.

Willie's maternal great-grandparents – Valentine McClure and Mary Jane Garrity

Willie's maternal great-grandfather Valentine McClure was born around 1876 in Glasgow to his uniquely named father Holt McClure, a labourer, and mother Mary Ann Harrison. His great-grandmother Mary Jane Garrity was also born around 1876 in Glasgow to father John Garrity, a shoemaker, and mother Helen Trainer. Valentine McClure, 20, a hammerman, of 34 Carrick Street, Anderston, Glasgow, married Mary Jane Garrity, 20, a paper store worker, of 7 Wood Lane, Glasgow, on 3 April 1896 at 46 St Vincent Crescent, Glasgow. The wedding was conducted by Rev George G Green, minister of the United Presbyterian Church; the best man was John McDonald and the best maid was Bella Garrity, Mary Jane's sister.

Valentine and Mary Jane had two known children in the Broomielaw, in the bustling docklands of Glasgow's River Clyde; daughter Helen (b. ~1898) and son George (b. 1900). In 1901, Valentine McClure, 25, a blacksmith's hammerman, resided at Back Land, 75 Brown Street, Broomielaw, Glasgow, with wife Mary Jane, 25, a shirt machinist, children Helen, 3, and George, 1. Also boarding there was Valentine's Irish stepfather Alexander Clarke, 56, a dock labourer, and his Irish-born mother Mary Ann Clarke, given as 48, a washerwoman. Valentine, a hammerman, and Mary Jane were both dead by 1922.

Willie's maternal great-grandparents – William Costley and Catherine Rankin

Willie's other maternal great-grandfather William Costley and great-grandmother Catherine Rankin were both born around 1875 in Glasgow. William Costley, an engine keeper, married Catherine Rankin and they had a daughter Rosina (b. ~1903) in Anderston, Glasgow. William, an engine keeper, was dead by 1922, although, wife Catherine was still alive by then.

Willie's paternal great-great-grandparents – James Anderson and Agnes Aitken

Willie's paternal great-great-grandfather James Anderson and great-great-grandmother Agnes Aitken were both born around 1820 in Leith, Edinburgh. James Anderson, a ship carpenter journeyman, married Agnes Aitken and they had a son John (b. ~1850) in North Leith, Edinburgh. James, a ship carpenter, was dead by 1875, although, wife Agnes was still alive by then.

Willie's paternal great-great-grandparents – David Ritchie and Marion Crawford

Willie's other paternal great-great-grandfather David Ritchie and great-great-grandmother Marion Crawford were both born around 1820 in Dirleton, Haddingtonshire. David Ritchie, a master shoemaker, married Marion Crawford and they had a daughter Isabella Gordon Ritchie (b. ~1854) in Dirleton, Haddingtonshire. David, a master shoemaker, and wife Marion were both dead by 1875.

Willie's maternal great-great-grandparents – Holt McClure and Mary Ann Harrison

Willie's maternal great-great-grandfather Holt McClure was born around 1841 to father William McClure and his great-great-grandmother Mary Ann Harrison was born around 1843 to father Valentine Harrison both in County Down, Ulster, Ireland. The two families lived through the devastating Irish Potato Famine (1846-52) where it was estimated around 1 million Irish perished through destitution and starvation and at least a further 1 million migrated to Britain, Canada, USA, Australia and New Zealand.

Holt McClure, 21, married Mary Ann Harrison, 19, on 5 July 1862 at Donaghcloney, County Down and the witnesses were their two fathers, William McClure and Valentine Harrison. Holt and Mary Ann had four known children; Henry Robert (b. 21 January 1860, Moira, Down), Margaret Jane (b. 20 August 1865, Waringstown, Down), William Henry (b. 1 February 1871, Lurgan, Shankhill, Antrim) and Valentine (b. ~1875, Glasgow). Around the mid-1870s the McClure family migrated to Glasgow and Holt was employed as a labourer.

Holt McClure, a labourer, was dead by 1896, although, wife Mary Ann was still alive. Mary Ann remarried her second husband Irish-born Alexander Clarke, a dock labourer. In 1901, Mary Ann Clarke, given as 48, although more likely 58, a washerwoman, resided at Back Land, 75 Brown Street, Broomielaw, Glasgow, with her husband Alexander Clarke, 56, a dock labourer, son Valentine McClure, 25, a blacksmith's hammerman, daughter-in-law

Mary Jane, 25, a shirt machinist, grandchildren Helen, 3, and George, 1.

Willie's maternal great-great-grandparents – John Garrity and Helen Trainer

Willie's other maternal great-great-grandfather John Garrity and great-great-grandmother Helen Trainer were both born around 1845 in Ulster, Ireland. John Garrity, a shoemaker, married Helen Trainer and they had two known daughters in Glasgow; Mary Jane (b. ~1876) and Bella. John, a shoemaker, and wife Helen were both dead by 1896.

Willie's maternal great-great-great-grandfathers – William McClure and Valentine Harrison

Willie's maternal great-great-great-grandfathers William McClure and Valentine Harrison, aka Val, were born around 1810 in County Down, Ulster, Ireland. William McClure had a son Holt McClure (b. ~1841) and Valentine Harrison had a daughter Mary Ann Harrison (b. ~1843). William McClure and Valentine Harrison were both still alive in 1862 as witnesses at Holt and Mary Ann's wedding in Donaghcloney, County Down.

Part 2

The other Barça Bears players 1966 – 1967

Campaign medallists

CHAPTER 12

Gerry Neef (goalkeeper)

Honours as a Rangers player:
1 European Cup Winners' Cup
1 Scottish League Cup

The young Gerry Neef

Just over a year after the end of WWII, Klaus Gerhard Neef was born on 30 October 1946 in Hausham, Bavaria, Germany to father Paul Neef and mother Emmi Schultes. When Neef was still only two years old, the defeated German Third Reich was divided between West and East Germany on 23 May 1949. He grew up in the west during the period of the 'Cold War', which pitted the western democracies against the communist states, mainly the Soviet Union and China.

In his youth, he played for SV Hamborn and went on to play for amateur sides Duisburg FV and VfvB Ruhrort / Laar. While playing at amateur level Gerhard was working as a German policeman, when he met future Scottish-born wife Marcia Frances Tyson, daughter of a British serviceman based in West Germany. Klaus Gerhard Neef married Marcia

Frances Tyson on 7 June 1968 in Münchengladbach, North Rhine-Westphalia, West Germany. Gerhard and Marcia had two daughters born in Paisley, Renfrewshire and the family lived in Penilee and Crookston.

Often known as Gerhard, he became a German professional football player, and he was known as Gerry during his career in Scotland. Although he was originally brought to Scotland by Eddie Turnbull, manager of Aberdeen, Neef was best known for his spell at Glasgow Rangers, where he signed in the spring of 1968. Neef was seen as the answer to the club's problematic goalkeeping position. Manager Davie White had been struggling to find a replacement to Billy Ritchie since his departure in 1967, using Erik Sorensen and Norrie Martin but remaining undecided about either.

Neef made his debut on 19 April 1969 in a league match against Greenock Morton, keeping a clean sheet in a 3-0 home win. Neef was in goal on that fateful, freezing night of 26 November 1969 when the author was taken to his first Rangers game at Ibrox along with his father Archie. Rangers lost 2-6 on aggregate to the Polish side Gornik Zabrze in the last 16 round of the ECWC. However, even after the sacking of Davie White following that defeat in favour of new manager Willie Waddell, Neef remained the first-choice goalkeeper at the club playing 39 games and winning the 1970 Scottish League Cup, after successfully keeping out Celtic in the final.

The 1970-71 season saw him lose his place to new signing Peter McCloy and his first-team appearances became sporadic after that. He was part of the 1971-72 European Cup Winners' Cup squad, and although he did not play in the campaign, he was the substitute goalkeeper on the bench in the Camp Nou when Rangers beat Dinamo Moscow 3-2, qualifying him for a winner's medal. While he was at Ibrox, Neef also volunteered as a football coach at nearby Cardonald Secondary School.

Neef left Rangers to return to West Germany in 1973, having made 48 appearances in total for the club. He played for FC Nürnberg from 1973-75 followed by a spell with FC Herzogenaurach from 1975-79. Neef remained the rest of his life in Nürnberg Südstadt and lived to see the reunification of East and West Germany on 3 October 1990, after the fall of the Berlin Wall the previous year. Klaus Gerhard Neef died in Nürnberg on 23 February 2010 and he was commemorated by the Old Firm fans with a minute's silence at Ibrox. This took place on 28 February 2010 when, fittingly, Maurice Edu's injury-time winner against Celtic all but sealed the league title for Rangers.

Gerry's parents – Paul Neef and Emma Schultes

Paul Neef was born in Potsdam, Brandenburg, Germany, near the capital Berlin. Potsdam was the site of the palatial residences of the Prussian Emperors and Kaiser Wilhelm until 1918. However, the Neef family later moved and Paul grew up in Oberhausen in the Ruhr valley, situated between Duisburg and Essen. Emma Schultes, aka Emmi, was born in Hausham, Bavaria, where she and Paul married.

Paul and Emmi had three known sons; Klaus Gerhard Neef, aka Gerry, Oliver Neef and Wolfgang Neef. Eldest son Klaus Gerhard Neef was born on 30 October 1946 in Hausham, Bavaria, Germany. Following the end of WWII, the Third Reich was dismantled by the United Nations and Germany was divided into East and West Germany on 23 May 1949. After schooling, Paul and Emmi's son Gerry became a policeman and then a professional football player, including spells in Scotland with Aberdeen and Rangers. Their son Oliver Neef became a scientist and son Wolfgang Neef became a businessman.

CHAPTER 13

Jim Denny (Defender)

Honours as a Rangers player:
1 European Cup Winners' Cup

The young Jim Denny

James Denny was born on 13 March 1950 at Barshaw Hospital, Paisley, Renfrewshire to father Duncan Denny, a pipe jointer, and mother Mary Thomas Lauchlan Quail. At that time the Denny family lived at 27 Maxwellton Street, Paisley. Denny was a professional football player and he joined Rangers in 1970 from junior side Yoker Athletic. He made his debut in the Scottish Cup final replay against Celtic on 12 May 1971. He played at right-back in place of the injured Sandy Jardine, but Rangers lost the match 2-1.

In total, he made 54 appearances for Rangers including the first match of the 1971-72 European Cup Winners' Cup campaign, a 1-1 draw with Stade Rennes. He was on the bench in Barcelona at the victorious ECWC final. He left Ibrox in 1977 after seven seasons and joined Hearts. He played more games in Edinburgh in two seasons than he had in the seven seasons he was at Rangers. His spell at Tynecastle was followed by a final season at Stirling Albion in 1981-82 before leaving the senior ranks to join Irvine Victoria.

Jim's parents – Duncan Denny and Mary Thomas Lauchlan Quail

Jim's father Duncan Denny was born on 11 December 1926 at 51 Canal Street, Paisley to father Duncan Denny, an engineer's labourer, and mother Annie Brown. Canal Street in Paisley lies at the end of the Paisley Canal railway line. The Glasgow, Paisley and Ardrossan Canal was opened in 1810 and did not stretch any further than the Johnstone basin. With the introduction of the railway system in the 1830s, the canal failed to be consistently profitable and was bought over by the Glasgow & South Western Railway Coy. The G&SWR operated it as a canal, mainly for freight traffic, but in 1886 it was converted to rail traffic. It is still affectionately known to this day as the Paisley Canal line.

Jim's mother Mary Thomas Lauchlan Quail was born on 1 February 1928 at 8 Galloway Street, Paisley to father Thomas Andrew Quail, a dyer's labourer, and mother Jeanie McLeod Wallace. Duncan Denny, 22, a Gas Department labourer, of 202 Ferguslie Park Avenue, Paisley, married Mary Thomas Lauchlan Quail, 20, a thread mill worker at J & P Coats, of 10 Logan Drive, Paisley, on 9 February 1949. The wedding was conducted by Rev G J Davidson Kelly, minister of St Ninian's Church of Scotland; the best man was James Denny,

Duncan's brother, and the best maid was Elizabeth Quail, Mary's sister. Son James Denny was born on 13 March 1950 at Barshaw Hospital, Paisley, Renfrewshire to father Duncan Denny, a pipe jointer, and mother Mary Thomas Lauchlan Quail. At that time the Denny family lived at 27 Maxwellton Street, Paisley.

Jim's paternal grandparents – Duncan Denny and Annie Brown

Jim's paternal grandfather Duncan Denny was born on 11 May 1895 at 19 Lawn Street, Paisley to father James Denny, a lithographer's labourer, and mother Maggie Gilchrist. His grandmother Annie Brown was born around 1902 in Paisley to father Alexander Brown, a carter, and mother Mary Ann Flanagan. Duncan Denny, 26, an engineer's labourer, of 27 Espedair Street, Paisley, married Annie Brown, 19, a thread mill worker at J & P Coats, of 57 Canal Street, Paisley, on 24 June 1921 at the South UF Manse. The wedding was conducted by Rev C J T Merrylees, minister of South United Free Church of Scotland; the witnesses were A Stewart and M Denny. Duncan and Annie had two known sons in Paisley; Duncan and James. Son Duncan Denny was born on 11 December 1926 at 51 Canal Street, Paisley. Duncan, a dyer's labourer, and Annie were still alive in 1949 at 202 Ferguslie Park Avenue, Paisley.

Jim's maternal grandparents – Thomas Andrew Quail and Jeanie McLeod Wallace

Jim's maternal grandfather Thomas Andrew Quail was born about 1899 in Paisley to father William Quail, a dyer, and mother Margaret Thomas. His grandmother Jeanie McLeod Wallace was born about 1903 in Paisley to father David Wallace, a hammerman, and mother Elizabeth McLeod. Thomas Andrew Quail, 22, a steelwork labourer, of 26 Lady Lane, Paisley, married Jeanie McLeod Wallace, 19, a thread mill worker at J & P Coats, of 28 Great Hamilton Street, Paisley, on 7 October 1921 at St Mary's Roman Catholic Chapel, Paisley. The wedding was conducted by Fr William Davidson; the best man was Michael Farmer, and the best maid was Mary McGrory.

Thomas and Jeanie had two known daughters in Paisley; Mary and Elizabeth. Daughter Mary Thomas Lauchlan Quail was born on 1 February 1928 at 8 Galloway Street, Paisley to father Thomas Andrew Quail, a dyer's labourer, and mother Jeanie McLeod Wallace. Thomas, an electric crane man, was dead by 1949 and his wife Jeanie had remarried a second husband named Somerville.

Jim's paternal great-grandparents - James Denny and Margaret Gilchrist

Jim's paternal great-grandfather James Denny (or Denney) was born on 26 January 1861 at 6 Cotton Street, Abbey, Paisley to father David Denny, a shawl weaver, and mother Jane Ferguson. His great-grandmother Margaret Gilchrist, aka Maggie, was born around 1867 in Paisley to father

Robert Gilchrist, another shawl weaver, and mother Susan Craig.

James Denny, 19, a lithographer's hand, of 19 Lawn Street, Paisley, married first wife Jeanie Donnelly, 21, a thread mill worker, who signed with her 'x' mark, of 3 Lawn Street, Paisley, on 26 November 1880 at 14 Mossvale Street, Paisley. The wedding was conducted by Rev Frederick Charles Niven, minister of the North Parish Church of Scotland; the best man was Henry Bickerstaff and the best maid was Mary McNeil. Tragically, James's wife Jeanie was dead by 1886 and he remarried his second wife Margaret Gilchrist.

James Denny, 25, a lithographer's hand, still at 19 Lawn Street, Paisley, married second wife Margaret Gilchrist, 19, a thread mill worker, of 76 George Street, Paisley, on 2 April 1886. The wedding was conducted by Rev W McIndoe, minister of the Free Church of Scotland; the witnesses were A Morrison and E Alexander. James and Maggie had two known sons; Duncan and James. Son Duncan Denny was born on 11 May 1895 at 19 Lawn Street, Paisley to father James Denny, a lithographer's labourer, and mother Maggie Gilchrist. James and Maggie were both still alive in 1921 in Paisley.

Jim's maternal great-grandparents - William Quail and Margaret Thomas

Jim's maternal great-grandfather William Quail and great-grandmother Margaret Thomas were both born about 1870 in Paisley. William Quail, a dyer, married Margaret

Thomas and they had a son Thomas Andrew Quail (b. ~1899). William, a dyer, was dead by 1921 and his wife Margaret had remarried by then.

Jim's maternal great-grandparents – David Wallace and Elizabeth McLeod

Jim's maternal great-grandfather David Wallace and great-grandmother Elizabeth McLeod were both born about 1875 in Paisley. David Wallace, a hammerman, married Elizabeth McLeod and they had a daughter Jeanie McLeod Wallace (b. ~1903) in Paisley. David, a hammerman, and Elizabeth were still alive in 1921.

Although the famed Wallace surname has been carried by emigrating Scots around the globe, it is a common Renfrewshire and Strathclyde surname. The name was given by the invading Romans to the Britons calling them the 'walensis' meaning 'foreigners'. The Britons were pushed west into Wales and north into Strathclyde. The renowned Scottish knight Sir William Wallace, of 'Braveheart' fame, has a monument erected at Elderslie near Paisley proclaiming his birthplace. This is a bit of a popular misconception as the Wallace lands were actually at the similarly named Ellerslie near Kilmaurs and Riccarton near Kilmarnock in Ayrshire and Auchinbothie near Lochwinnoch, all a few miles to the south. The misconception of Elderslie first appears in a 17th-century poem by the bard Blind Harry.

> *Elderslie then had in heritage,*
> *Auchinbothie, and other sundry place,*

The great-grandson he was of good Wallace,
The which Wallace full worthily then wrought.

Jim's paternal great-great-grandparents – David Denny and Jane Ferguson

Jim's paternal great-great-grandfather David Denny (or Denney) and great-great-grandmother Jane Ferguson were both born around 1830 in Paisley. David Denny became one of the many shawl weavers in Paisley, the town becoming famed for its elaborate paisley-pattern shawls exported around the world. David Denny, a shawl weaver, married Jane Ferguson and they had a son James Denny born on 26 January 1861 at 6 Cotton Street, Abbey parish in Paisley. David, a shawl weaver, and wife Jane were both still alive in 1886 in Paisley.

Jim's paternal great-great-grandparents – Robert Gilchrist and Susan Craig

Jim's other paternal great-great-grandfather Robert Gilchrist and great-great-grandmother Susan Craig were born around 1835 in Paisley. Robert Gilchrist, another shawl weaver, married Susan Craig and they had a daughter Margaret, aka Maggie (b. ~1867) in Paisley. Robert, a shawl weaver, was still alive in 1886, although, his wife Susan was dead by then.

CHAPTER 14

Graham Fyfe (Winger)

Honours as a Rangers player:
1 European Cup Winners' Cup

The young Graham Fyfe

G raham Ellerby Fyfe was born on 18 August 1951 at 14 Linksview Road, Motherwell, Lanarkshire to father William McKenzie Fyfe, a motor lorry driver, and mother Susan Beck O'Neill. He was a professional football player, best known for his time with Rangers. Fyfe made his first appearance for Rangers at Ibrox in a league match against Hearts on 25 March 1969. He started on the right-wing in a 3-2 home win. He went on to make 70 appearances for the club, including being on the bench for the 1972 ECWC final in Barcelona. He also played in the first tie against Ajax Amsterdam in the inaugural European Super Cup. Fyfe also scored 23 goals for Rangers, a creditable tally from a midfielder.

In 1976 he left to join Hibernian after seven seasons at Ibrox, but his stay in Edinburgh was short-lived, as he moved on to Dumbarton the following year. He played at Boghead Park for two seasons from 1977-79, before moving to the USA to play with the Major Indoor Soccer League sides Pittsburgh Spirit and Cleveland Force. In 1980 Fyfe stated publicly that he had to leave Rangers because he had married his wife, a Roman Catholic, although this was denied by the club. In 1983 Fyfe signed with the St Louis Steamers and spent one season with them, bringing his playing career to an end.

Graham's parents – William McKenzie Fyfe and Susan Beck O'Neill

Graham's father William McKenzie Fyfe was born on 11 December 1910 in the Gartsherrie Institute House, Coatbridge, Lanarkshire to father William McKenzie Fyfe, the Institute's janitor, and mother Isabella Crosbie. Graham's mother Susan Beck O'Neill, also recorded as Annie, was born on 2 June 1908 at 7 Chapel Square, Chapel, Cambusnethan to father John O'Neill, a coal miner, and mother Ellen McGurk. In 1911, Susan, aka Annie, 3, resided at 30 Morningside Square, Cambusnethan, with her father John O'Neill, 31, a coal miner drawer, mother Nellie, 30, and her other siblings.

William McKenzie Fyfe, 22, an omnibus conductor, of 30 Caledonian Road, Wishaw, married Susan Beck O'Neill, 25, a domestic servant, of 12 Northmuir Drive, Cambusnethan, on 29 September 1933 at St Ignatius RC Church, Wishaw. The wedding was conducted by Fr Thomas J Murray, the

Rectory, Wishaw; the best man was John O'Neill, Susan's brother, and the best maid was Mary O'Neill, Susan's sister-in-law. Son Graham Ellerby Fyfe was born on 18 August 1951 at 14 Linksview Road, Motherwell, Lanarkshire to father William McKenzie Fyfe, a motor lorry driver, and mother Susan Beck O'Neill.

Graham's paternal grandparents – William McKenzie Fyfe and Isabella Crosbie

Graham's paternal grandfather William McKenzie Fyfe was born on 26 April 1876 at Muirhouses, Kirriemuir, Forfarshire, to father Alexander Fyfe, a ploughman, and mother Jessie Ogilvie. In 1891, William, 14, a farm servant, resided at Cirkston Cottage, Airlie, Kirriemuir, with his father Alexander Fyfe, 47, a farm servant, mother Jessie, 48, and sister Jane, 10. Graham's grandmother Isabella Crosbie was born around 1877 in Dumfriesshire to father James Crosbie, a van man, and mother Sarah Kennedy.

William Fyfe, 22, a grocer, of 21 Castle Street, Dumfries, married Isabella Crosbie, 21, of 39 Loreburn Street, Dumfries, on 15 June 1898 at Greyfriars Manse, Dumfries. The wedding was conducted by Rev Robert Wilkie, minister of Greyfriars Parish Church of Scotland; the best man was James Crosbie and the best maid was Maud Crosbie. Son William McKenzie Fyfe was born on 11 December 1910 in the Gartsherrie Institute House, Coatbridge, Lanarkshire to father William, the Gartsherrie Institute's janitor, and mother Isabella. William McKenzie Fyfe senior, the Institute's janitor, was dead by 1933, although, his wife Isabella was still alive by then.

Gartsherrie Institute was built by William Baird & Coy for recreation and education of their predominantly Protestant workforce. Bairds were centred in Gartsherrie, Coatbridge and the directors were staunchly Protestant and politically Conservative. By 1840, Bairds' Eglinton Iron Works produced 25% of Scotland's pig iron. Bairds played a pro-active role in bringing migrants from Ulster to Scotland; attracting workers by advertising in Belfast, promising housing and schooling.

Education was considered essential in instilling the employers' values in their community, importantly including religious studies. Bairds used the mediums of sport, recreation, and education to build a sense of solidarity amongst their workforce. The firm built Institutes at Kilwinning, Lugar, Muirkirk, Gartsherrie and Twechar. The Gartsherrie Institute had swimming pools and a reading room, encouraging company musical bands and Total Abstinence Societies.

Bairds also gave their patronage to junior football clubs like Kilwinning Rangers and Larkhall Thistle. If social control was the aim of this sporting patronage, it is impossible to analyse its relative 'successes' in forcing local footballers to accept the moral perspective of their patrons. Footballers and supporters in these communities were pre-disposed to support Protestant organisations such as Rangers. As Catholics faced discrimination from Protestant workplaces and cultural spheres, it was logical that they too would gravitate towards Catholic associations.

It may be difficult to evaluate the relative success of sporting patronage given by firms such as Bairds of Gartsherrie, but this paternalism was nevertheless indelibly linked to migration from Ireland, and the need to formulate a common Protestant identity between owners and workers.

Graham's maternal grandparents – John O'Neill and Ellen McGurk

Graham's maternal grandfather John O'Neill (or O'Neil) was born around 1880 in Cambusnethan, Lanarkshire to father Andrew O'Neill, a coal miner, and mother Margaret Bryson. John would follow his father into the bowels of the Lanarkshire coalfields. His grandmother Ellen McGurk, aka Nellie, was born around 1881 in Cambusnethan to father John McGurk, a blast furnaceman, and mother Annie Beck.

John O'Neill, 23, a coal miner, of 144 Cleland's Land, Cambusnethan, married Ellen McGurk, 23, a farm servant, of Moss Street, Cambusnethan, on 15 July 1904 at St Ignatius Church, Wishaw. The wedding was conducted by Fr John Leonard, Roman Catholic clergyman; the best man was James Caffrey and the best maid was Mary Macguire.

John and Ellen had seven known children in Cambusnethan, although one died in infancy; Nellie (b. ~1900), John (b. ~1905), Patrick (b. ~1907), Susan Beck, aka Annie (b. 2 June 1908), twins Edward McGurk and Maggie Bryson (b. 9 September 1910). Daughter Susan Beck O'Neill was born on 2 June 1908 at 7 Chapel Square, Chapel, Cambusnethan. In 1911, John O'Neill, 31, a coal miner drawer, resided at 30 Morningside Square, Cambusnethan, with wife Nellie, 30, children Nellie, 11, and John, 6, both scholars, Patrick, 4, Susan, aka Annie, 3, and twins Edward and Maggie, 6 months old. Also boarding at John's home was his Whifflet-born brother-in-law Edward McGurk, 21, a coal miner drawer. John and Ellen were still alive in 1933 in Cambusnethan.

Graham's paternal great-grandparents – Alexander Fyfe and Jessie Ogilvie

Graham's paternal great-grandfather Alexander Fyfe was born on 31 January 1842 at Haugh of Coupar Grange, Bendochy, Perthshire to father Alexander Fyfe, a farm servant, and mother Isabella Davie. His great-grandmother Jessie Ogilvie (or Ogilvy) was born around 1843 in Fearn, Forfarshire to father Thomas Ogilvie, a labourer, and mother Mary Simpson. Alexander Fyfe, 28, a ploughman, of Reedie, Airlie, Kirriemuir, married Jessie Ogilvie, 28, a domestic servant, of Littleton, Airlie, on 31 May 1872 at Northmuir, Kirriemuir. The wedding was conducted by Rev John A Murray, minister of Kirriemuir United Presbyterian; the best man was Alan McDonald and the best maid was Susan Ogilvie, Jessie's sister.

Alexander and Jessie had two known children; William McKenzie (b. 26 April 1876, Kirriemuir) and Jane (b. ~1881, Glamis). Son William McKenzie Fyfe was born on 26 April 1876 at Muirhouses, Kirriemuir. In 1891, Alexander Fyfe, 47, a farm servant, resided at Cirkston Cottage, Airlie, with wife Jessie, 48, son William, 14, a farm servant, and daughter Jane, 10. Alexander, stated as a farmer, and Jessie were both still alive in 1898 in Kirriemuir.

Graham's paternal great-grandparents – James Crosbie and Sarah Kennedy

Graham's paternal great-grandfather James Crosbie and great-grandmother Sarah Kennedy were both born around 1850 in Dumfriesshire. James Crosbie married Sarah Kennedy and they had three known children; James, Isabella (b. ~1877) and Maud. Daughter Isabella Crosbie was born around 1877 in Dumfriesshire. James Crosbie, a van man, was still alive in 1898, although his wife Sarah was dead by then.

Graham's maternal great-grandparents – Andrew O'Neill and Margaret Bryson

Graham's maternal great-grandfather Andrew O'Neill and great-grandmother Margaret Bryson were both born around 1850 and almost certainly of Irish ancestry. Andrew O'Neill, a coal miner, married Margaret Bryson and they had a son John (b. ~1880) in Cambusnethan, Lanarkshire. Andrew, a coal miner, and wife Margaret were still alive in 1904.

Graham's maternal great-grandparents – John McGurk and Annie Beck

Graham's maternal great-grandfather John McGurk and great-grandmother Annie Beck were both born around 1850 and almost certainly of Irish ancestry. John McGurk, a blast furnaceman, married Annie Beck and they had a daughter Ellen, aka Nellie (b. ~1881) in Cambusnethan, Lanarkshire. John, a blast furnaceman, and wife Annie were still alive in 1904.

Graham's paternal great-great-grandparents – Alexander Fyfe and Isabella Davie

Graham's paternal great-great-grandfather Alexander Fyfe and great-great-grandmother Isabella Davie, aka Isabel, were both born around 1815 in Bendochy, Perthshire. Alexander Fyfe, a farm servant, married Isabella Davie and they had a son Alexander (b. 31 January 1842) at Haugh of Coupar Grange, Bendochy. The birth is recorded in the OPRs for the parish of Bendochy as follows:-

> *OPR Births Bendochy 332/3/27*
>
> *1842: Alexander lawful son of Alexander Fyfe and Isabel Davie, Haugh of Coupar Grange, was born 31st January and baptized 26th February 1842: Fyfe*

Alexander, a farm servant, was still alive in 1872, although, his wife Isabella was dead by then.

Graham's paternal great-great-grandparents – Thomas Ogilvie and Mary Simpson

Graham's paternal great-great-grandfather Thomas Ogilvie and great-great-grandmother Mary Simpson were both born around 1815 in Fearn, Forfarshire. Thomas Ogilvie, a labourer, married Mary Simpson and they had two known daughters in Fearn; Jessie (b. ~1844) and Susan. Thomas, a labourer, and wife Mary were both still alive in 1872.

CHAPTER 15

Andy Penman (Midfielder)

Honours as a Rangers player:
1 European Cup Winners' Cup

The young Andy Penman

Andrew Penman was born on 20 February 1943 at 68 Middlebank Street, Rosyth, Fife to father James Penman, a slater, and mother Alexina Gordon Smith. He was a professional footballer, who played for Dundee, Rangers and Arbroath. Penman started his career at Dens Park and helped Dundee win the Scottish League championship in 1962 alongside great players like Alan Gilzean. While at Dundee, he gained his only Scotland cap in a 3-0 defeat to the Netherlands on 11 May 1966 and also represented the Scottish League XI six times. He moved to Rangers in 1967 under manager Davie White.

Penman was also playing in midfield on that fateful, freezing night of 26 November 1969 when the author went to his first game with his father Archie. Rangers lost 2-6 on aggregate to

Gornik Zabrze. He played at Ibrox for five seasons and he was a substitute in Barcelona for the 1972 European Cup Winners' Cup final. He left Rangers soon after to join Arbroath later in 1972. After leaving Arbroath in 1976, Penman played for Inverness Caledonian in the Highland League before retiring from football. Penman is revered at Dundee and there is a lounge at Dens Park named in his honour.

Andy's parents – James Penman and Alexina Gordon Smith

Andy's father James Penman was born on Burns' Day, 25 January 1907 at Tenement 2/1 Dr Begg's Buildings, Canongate, Edinburgh to father James Penman, a railway parcels deliverer, and mother Helen Calder Hammond. His mother Alexina Gordon Smith was born on 18 August 1907 at 62 Virginia Street, St Nicholas, Aberdeen to father James Riddell Smith, a shipwright journeyman, and mother Charlotte Ann Tawse Forbes. In 1911, James, 4, still resided at Tenement 2/1, Dr Begg's Buildings, Canongate, Edinburgh, with his father James Penman, 37, a union room labourer at a brewery, mother Helen, 38, siblings Agnes, 11, and Maggie, 9, both at school, and Helen, 9 months old. After schooling, James became an apprentice slater and Alexina took a job as an assistant in a general store when her family moved to Rosyth in Fife.

James Penman, 28, a slater, of 51 Holburn Place, Rosyth, married Alexina Gordon Smith, 28, of 25 Parkside Street, Rosyth, on 28 September 1935 at Rosyth Church of

Scotland. The wedding was conducted by Rev Arnold Boyd; the best man was John Turnbull and the best maid was Ellen Smith, Alexina's sister. Son Andrew Penman was born on 20 February 1943 at 68 Middlebank Street, Rosyth.

Andy's paternal grandparents – James Penman and Helen Calder Hammond

Andy's paternal grandfather James Penman was born on 25 February 1874 at Old Town, Dollar, Clackmannanshire, to father James Penman, a miner, and mother Margaret Tulloch. His grandmother Helen Calder Hammond was born on 15 October 1872 in the army barracks of Edinburgh Castle at the top of the Royal Mile, Edinburgh, to father Daniel Hammond, a sergeant in the 93rd Regiment of Foot, the Sutherland Highlanders, and mother Agnes Duncan.

After schooling, James was employed by the North British Railway Company in Edinburgh as a railway parcels deliverer and Helen, like many young girls of the Victorian Era, went into domestic service. James Penman, 24, a railway parcels deliverer, of 8 Comely Green Place, Abbeyhill, Edinburgh, married Helen Calder Hammond, 25, of 17 St James Street, Saint Andrew, Edinburgh, on 7 October 1898 at Helen's family home. The wedding was conducted by Rev James W Sinclair, minister of St James Place United Presbyterian Church; the best man was William Penman, James's brother, and the best maid was called Margaret.

James and Helen had four known children in Edinburgh; Agnes (b.~1900), Maggie (b.~1902), James (b. 25 January 1907) and Helen (b. ~1910). Son James Penman was born on 25 January 1907 at Tenement 2/1 Dr Begg's Buildings, Canongate, Edinburgh. The Reverend Dr Begg constructed various tenements in the late 19th century as part of 'co-operative colonies' to improve the housing conditions for the working-classes in various parts of Edinburgh, such as Canongate, South Leith and Abbeyhill. In 1911, James Penman, 37, a union room labourer at a brewery, resided at Tenement 2/1 Dr Begg's Buildings, Canongate, Edinburgh, with wife Helen, 38, children Agnes, 11, and Maggie, 9, both at school, James, 4, and Helen, 9 months old.

James worked at the nearby Canongate Brewery. The Canongate Brewery was established by William Aitchison & Coy, who moved their brewing operations to Edinburgh from the Kerfield Brewery in Peebles in 1828. A new partnership, John Aitchison & Coy, was established to run the brewery and was established in 1895.

In 1935 James Penman was an aerodrome storekeeper, at Rosyth airfield, which was there to protect the strategically important Royal Naval dockyards. James's wife Helen was also still alive in 1935 in Rosyth.

Andy's maternal grandparents – James Riddell Smith and Charlotte Ann Tawse Forbes

Andy's maternal grandfather James Riddell Smith was born illegitimately around 1882 in St Nicholas, Aberdeen to mother Margaret Smith. The 'father of repute' is unknown, however, there is a strong possibility that he was called James Riddell, as a woman would name and shame the errant father using the child's name. His grandmother Charlotte Ann Tawse Forbes was born around 1882 in St Nicholas, Aberdeen to father John Mack Forbes, a seaman in the Merchant Service, and mother Margaret Tawse. After schooling both worked in the bustling docks of Aberdeen, James became an apprentice shipwright and Charlotte worked as a fish worker, one of the fabled 'Aiberdeen fishwives'.

James Riddell Smith, 23, a shipwright journeyman, of 12 Links Street, Aberdeen, married Charlotte Ann Tawse Forbes, 23, a fish worker, of 41 Miller Street, Aberdeen, on 15 December 1905 at 16 Broad Street, Aberdeen. The wedding was conducted by Rev Charles Cadell Macdonald, minister of St Clement's Church of Scotland; the best man was James Main and the best maid was Maggie Harrows. James and Charlotte had two known daughters in Aberdeen; Alexina Gordon (b. 18 August 1907) and Ellen. Daughter Alexina Gordon Smith was born on 18 August 1907 at 62 Virginia Street, St Nicholas, Aberdeen.

By 1935 James, a shipwright, had moved his family to 25 Parkside Street, Rosyth, Fife, and he was working in the militarily strategic Rosyth Royal Naval dockyards. James's wife Charlotte was dead by 1935.

Andy's paternal great-grandparents – James Penman and Margaret Tulloch

Andy's paternal great-grandfather James Penman was born around 1854 in Dollar, Clackmannanshire, Scotland's smallest county, to father James Penman, a coal miner, and mother Helen Wilson. His grandmother Margaret Tulloch was born around 1853 in Tillicoultry, Clackmannanshire to father William Tulloch, a labourer, and mother Margaret Blackwood.

James Penman, 19, a coal miner, of Sheardale, Dollar, married Margaret Tulloch, 20, of 38 Mill Street, Tillicoultry, on New Years' Day, 1 January 1873 at Margaret's family home. The wedding was conducted by Rev David Smith, of Tillicoultry Church of Scotland; the best man was Dougal Turner and the best maid was Mary Bonar. Son James Penman was born on 25 February 1874 at Old Town, Dollar, Clackmannanshire. James, a railway inspector with the North British Railway Company, and wife Margaret were still alive in 1898 in Edinburgh.

Andy's paternal great-grandparents – Daniel Hammond and Agnes Duncan

Andy's other paternal great-grandfather Daniel Hammond was born on 17 May 1837 in Inveresk, Haddingtonshire to father Daniel Hammond, a farm servant, and mother Margaret Thomson. The birth is recorded in the OPRs for the parish of Inveresk and Musselburgh as follows:-

> *OPR Births Inveresk and Musselburgh 689/15/485*
> *1837: Daniel Hammond, farm servant, and Margaret*
> *Thomson his wife, their son Daniel born 17th May and*
> *baptized 25th May 1837. Witnesses Alexander Lauder*
> *and James Johnson*

Andy's great-grandmother Agnes Duncan was born around 1846 in Edinburgh, Midlothian to father Peter Duncan, a ploughman, and mother Helen Calder. After schooling, Agnes went into domestic service. In 1851, Daniel Hammond, 13, a gardener's servant, resided at Bainfield House, St Cuthbert's, Edinburgh at the home of James Smail, 48, a market gardener, and his family.

Bainfield House was built in the early 19th century to a 2-storey, 3-bay rectangular-plan, being a symmetrical classical house set back within a formal garden area. The 1853 Ordnance Survey map labels this property 'Bainfield House'. The map also shows a formal parterre to the rear and a double-circular drive to the front. A small summer house was set against the north boundary and a pump-house lay behind the house. It is a British Listed Building and is now called Baynefield House at 122 Ferry Road, Edinburgh.

Daniel Hammond enlisted in the 93rd Regiment of Foot. The regiment sailed for India and arrived in Calcutta in September 1857, immediately being thrown into action during the Indian Mutiny. In 1861 the regiment was renamed the 93rd Regiment of Foot, Sutherland Highlanders, and returned from India by early 1870. Daniel rose to the rank of sergeant. By 1870 Agnes Duncan was working as a domestic servant living below stairs at No.9 Abercromby Place, Edinburgh in the fashionable Stockbridge district.

Daniel Hammond, 32, a sergeant in the 93rd Regiment, Sutherland Highlanders, residing at Perth Barracks, married Agnes Duncan, 24, a domestic servant, of No.9 Abercromby Place, Edinburgh, on 4 February 1870 at 271 South Street, James Street, Edinburgh. The wedding was conducted by Rev Andrew

Gardiner, officiating minister of the United Presbyterian Church; the best man was Alexander Duncan, Agnes's brother, and the best maid was Ann Murray. Daughter Helen Calder Hammond was born on 15 October 1872 in the army barracks of Edinburgh Castle at the top of the Royal Mile, Edinburgh, to father Daniel Hammond, a sergeant in the 93rd Regiment of Foot, Sutherland Highlanders, and mother Agnes Duncan.

Daniel left the army and got a job as a railway gatekeeper with the North British Railway Company, however, his employment was short-lived as he fell ill with bronchitis in 1875. Daniel Hammond, only 39, a railway gatekeeper, died on 29 August 1876 at 1 Friar Street Terrace, St George, Edinburgh, of chronic bronchitis, for 1 year, as certified by Dr John Lintore MD. The death was registered by his brother William Hammond, of 12 Upper Grove Place, Edinburgh. Daniel's wife Agnes was still alive in 1898 in Edinburgh.

Andy's maternal great-grandmother – Margaret Smith

Andy's maternal great-grandmother Margaret Smith was born around 1860 in Aberdeen. Margaret had a son James Riddell Smith born illegitimately around 1882 in St Nicholas, Aberdeen. The 'father of repute' is unknown, however, there is a strong possibility that he was called James Riddell, as it was common for a woman to name and shame the errant father in the naming of the child. Margaret Smith later married husband John Robertson, a school caretaker, and she was still alive in 1905.

Andy's maternal great-grandparents – John Mack Forbes and Margaret Tawse

Andy's maternal great-grandfather John Mack Forbes and his great-grandmother Margaret Tawse were both born around 1855 in Aberdeenshire. After schooling, John became a seaman in the Merchant Service. Margaret's surname of Tawse is unusual and comes from the Scots word 'tawse' which was effectively a hard leather strap, generally used by a schoolteacher to instil discipline. Many of the author's generation will still remember having to get 'the belt', although this only happened to him on only one occasion at Allan Glen's School. John Mack Forbes, a seaman, married Margaret Tawse and they had two known children in St Nicholas, Aberdeen; Charlotte Ann Tawse Forbes (b. ~1882) and William James Hay Forbes (b. 7 November 1891).

John Mack Forbes, a seaman in the Merchant Service, was deceased by 1905. In a newspaper obituary notice as follows: Margaret Forbes nee Tawse died on 26 July 1917, during WWI. On that same Thursday, Royal Navy cruiser HMS Ariadne was sunk in the English Channel by German submarine UC-65 with the loss of 38 crew members.

Andy's paternal great-great-grandparents – James Penman and Helen Wilson

Andy's paternal great-great-grandfather James Penman was born on 27 September 1827 in Dollar, Clackmannanshire. His great-great-grandmother Helen Wilson was born on 10 April 1828 in Dollar, Clackmannanshire. James Penman, a coal miner, married pregnant Helen Wilson on 12 June 1847 in Dollar and they had 13 known children in Dollar; Ann (b. 27 November 1847), William (b. 15 November 1849), James (b. ~1854), Thomas (b. 7 January 1857), George (b. 18 January 1859, died in infancy), Margaret (b. 8 April 1861), Helen (b. 2 May 1863), Janet (b. 5 March 1865), an unnamed daughter (b. 30 June 1867, died in infancy), twins Elizabeth and Jane (b. 26 July 1868), Mary (b. 26 September 1870) and Hugh (b. 17 March 1873, Sheardale, Dollar). James Penman, 79, a coal miner, died on 25 February 1907 in Dollar. Helen Penman nee Wilson, 86, died on 7 November 1914, during WWI, at Coalsnaughton, Clackmannanshire.

Andy's paternal great-great-grandparents – William Tulloch and Margaret Blackwood

Andy's other paternal great-great-grandfather William Tulloch was born in Garvald, Haddingtonshire around 1798. His great-great-grandmother Margaret Blackwood was born around 1816 in Dollar, Clackmannanshire. William Tulloch, a labourer, married first wife Margaret Watson on 13 July 1816 at Mountfair, Haddington. After Margaret Watson died he married second wife Margaret Blackwood and they had a daughter Margaret (b. ~1853) in Tillicoultry, Clackmannanshire. In 1861, William and Margaret were still living in Tillicoultry. William Tulloch, a labourer, died on 19 July 1866 at Garvald, Haddingtonshire. William's wife Margaret was still alive in 1873 in Tillicoultry.

Andy's paternal great-great-grandparents – Daniel Hammond and Margaret Thomson

Andy's other paternal great-great-grandfather Daniel Hammond and great-great-grandmother Margaret Thomson were both born around 1810 in Haddingtonshire. Daniel Hammond, a farm servant, married Margaret Thomson and they had two known sons in Inveresk; Daniel (b. 17 May 1837) and William. In 1870 Daniel was working as a provision's merchants van driver, which in those days would be a horse-drawn van. Daniel and wife Margaret were both still alive in 1876.

Andy's paternal great-great-grandparents – Peter Duncan and Helen Calder

Andy's other paternal great-great-grandfather Peter Duncan and great-great-grandmother Helen Calder were born around 1820 in Edinburgh, Midlothian. Peter Duncan, a ploughman, married Helen Calder and they had two known children in Edinburgh; Agnes (b. ~1846) and Alexander. Peter, a ploughman, and wife Helen were both still alive in 1820.

CHAPTER 16

Derek Parlane (Forward)

Honours as a Rangers player:
1 European Cup Winners' Cup
3 Scottish League titles
3 Scottish Cups
3 Scottish League Cups

The young Derek Parlane

Derek James Parlane was born on 5 May 1953 at Braeholm Maternity Hospital, Helensburgh, Dunbartonshire, to father James Parlane, a nurseryman, and mother Margaret Nichol Russell. At that time the Parlane family were living at Elimar, Rhu in Dunbartonshire. Derek's father Jimmy had also played at Ibrox as an inside forward in the Willie Waddell and Willie Thornton era, between 1945 and 1950, and his son Derek played at Ibrox as a striker. It is believed that they were the only father and son to have played for Rangers by that period. In 1970, Waddell signed Derek, and he and assistant manager Thornton visited market gardener Jimmy Parlane's home in Rhu to complete the signing. Parlane played for Rangers from 1970-80, winning three Scottish League championships, three Scottish Cups, three Scottish League Cups and a European Cup Winners' Cup. He was also capped twelve times for Scotland with one Under-21 cap.

He transferred to Leeds United in March 1980 but it was not a successful period. He scored 10 goals in 53 appearances for Leeds before going to Hong Kong on loan to Bulova. On 14 July 1983, new Manchester City manager Billy McNeill brought him to Maine Road. Parlane linked up with fellow Scot, Jim Tolmie, and on their debut for the Blues on 27 August 1983, City beat Crystal Palace 2-1 at Selhurst Park in the Second Division. Parlane and Tolmie each scored, setting a precedent for the rest of the season. Parlane scored 20 goals in 48 appearances for City.

Parlane was injured in September 1984 and was sold to Swansea Town in January 1985. After the season finished he played in New Zealand for the summer with North Shore United. He then spent the 1985-86 season in Belgium with Racing Jet, before returning to play two seasons with Rochdale from 1986-88, playing 42 games and scoring 10 times. His last professional club was Airdrieonians in the 1987-88 season, scoring 4 goals in 9 games, before finally signing for non-league club Macclesfield Town, where he finished his playing career.

Derek's parents – James Parlane and Margaret Nicholl Russell

Derek's father James Parlane was born on 12 February

1919 at Rosevale Cottage, Rhu, Dunbartonshire, to father Alexander Parlane, a nurseryman, and mother Isabella Bruce McKenzie. His mother Margaret Nicholl Russell was born on 24 September 1925 in Bangor, County Down, Ulster, Northern Ireland to father Frank Russell, a park ranger, and mother Sarah Caulfield.

Jimmy Parlane had also been a professional footballer like his son Derek and he was signed by Rangers from Queens Park. He played at inside forward in the famous era of Waddell, Thornton and Woodburn scoring his debut goal against Celtic on 7 September 1946 in the Scottish League. By season 1947-48 he was getting very little first-team football at Rangers and he was sold on to Airdrieonians where he finished his playing career.

James Parlane, 30, a nurseryman, married Margaret Nicholl Russell, 23, on 27 June 1949 in Bangor, County Down, Northern Ireland. Son Derek James Parlane was born on 5 May 1953 at Braeholm Maternity Hospital, Helensburgh. At that time the Parlane family were living at Elimar, Rhu, Dunbartonshire. Jimmy and Margaret also had a son Ian Parlane.

The tiny Dunbartonshire village of Rhu holds a special place in the history of Rangers. Rhu was the birthplace of Peter McNeil (1854-1901), a Scottish footballer, and his brother Moses McNeil (1855-1938), two of the founding fathers of Glasgow Rangers Football Club. Rhu was also the birthplace of Peter Campbell (~1858-1883), another Scottish footballer and founding father. Peter McNeil, Moses McNeil and Peter Campbell, along with William McBeath met at West End Park (now called Kelvingrove Park) in February 1872.

Rangers played their first match in May 1872, which was a goalless friendly draw with Callander on Glasgow Green.

In 1970, manager Willie Waddell and his assistant Willie Thornton visited market gardener Jimmy Parlane's home and signed his son Derek to play at Ibrox. A century after the foundation of the club, Jimmy's son Derek was a substitute on the bench in the Camp Nou in Barcelona for the victorious 1972 European Cup Winners' Cup final. James Parlane, 71, a nurseryman, died on 25 August 1990 at Rosevale, Cumberland Road, Rhu, as registered by son Ian Parlane at Helensburgh. His wife Margaret Nicholl Parlane nee Russell, 87, died on 13 August 2013 at the Vale of Leven Hospital, Alexandria, as registered by son Ian Parlane at Helensburgh.

Derek's paternal grandparents – Alexander Parlane and Isabella Bruce McKenzie

Derek's paternal grandfather Alexander Parlane was born on 9 July 1876 at Glebeside Row, Rhu, Dunbartonshire, to father William Parlane, a gardener, and mother Eliza Walker. In 1881, Alexander, 4, resided at Laurel Cottage, Rhu, with his father William Parlane, 39, a gardener, mother Eliza, 27, and his other siblings. His grandmother Isabella Bruce McKenzie was born around 1888 in Alvah, Banffshire, to father John McKenzie, a farmer, and mother Margaret Chalmers.

Alexander Parlane, 27, a florist, of Rosevale Cottage, Rhu, married Isabella Bruce McKenzie, 22, of Rosslea, Rhu, on 4 March 1904 at 21 Ravelston Park, Edinburgh. The wedding was conducted by Rev James Wilson, minister of

Dean Parish Church of Scotland; the best man was William Robertson and the best maid was Millie Allan. Son James Parlane was born on 12 February 1919 at Rosevale Cottage, Rhu, to father Alexander Parlane, a nurseryman, and mother Isabella Bruce McKenzie. Alexander, a nurseryman, and wife Isabella were both dead by 1990 as recorded on their son James's death certificate.

Derek's maternal grandparents – Frank Russell and Sarah Caulfield

Derek's maternal grandfather Frank Russell was born around 1897 in Belfast, County Antrim, Ireland, to father Thomas Russell, an iron moulder, and mother Elizabeth George. His grandmother Sarah Caulfield, aka Sadie, was born around 1896 in Bangor, County Down, Ireland, to father Robert Caulfield, a general contractor, and mother Margaret Nicholl. By 1909, Frank's mother Elizabeth had died and his father Thomas had remarried second wife Sarah Jane McKnight.

In 1911, Frank, 14, an assistant pawnbroker, resided at 13 Glencairn Street, Shankhill, West Belfast, with his father Thomas Russell, 45, an iron moulder, his stepmother Sarah Jane, 37, sister Catherine, 17, a seamstress, and stepbrother John McKnight, 9 months old. Also in 1911, Sarah, 15, resided at 28 Albert Street, Bangor, County Down, with her father Robert Caulfield, a general contractor, her mother Margaret, 36, and her other siblings. In 1912, in opposition to the British Government's highly contentious Home Rule Parliament Act, most Ulster Protestant men signed the Ulster

Covenant and women signed the Ulster Declaration. There appears no record of her father Robert signing the Covenant, however, Sadie Caulfield, of 28 Albert Street, Bangor, signed the Declaration at the Trinity Church Hall on Ulster Day, 28 September 1912.

After the end of WWI civil war broke out in Ireland (1919-20) with the Irish Republican Army conducting a guerrilla campaign designed to gain an independent Irish republic. Eventually, an agreement was reached under the Government of Ireland Act 1920, which separated the mainly Protestant northern province of Ulster into Northern Ireland on 3 May 1921 and the southern counties, which were mainly Catholic, into the Irish Free State in 1922. Northern Ireland remained part of the United Kingdom and the Irish Free State became the Republic of Ireland.

Frank Russell, a park ranger, married Sarah Caulfield and they had a daughter Margaret Nicholl Russell born on 24 September 1925 in Bangor, County Down, Ulster, Northern Ireland. Frank and wife Sarah were both dead by 2013 as recorded on their daughter Margaret's death certificate.

Derek's paternal great-grandparents – William Parlane and Eliza Ann Walker

Derek's paternal great-grandfather William Parlane was born on 1 February 1841 in Alexandria, parish of Bonhill, Dunbartonshire, to father James Parlane, a calico printer, and mother Agnes Wilson Smith. His great-grandmother Eliza Ann Walker was born around 1853 in Bromley, Middlesex,

England, to father Timothy John Walker, a sea captain, and mother Mary Gill. William Parlane, 27, a master gardener, of Kirk Park, Rhu, married Eliza Walker, 18, of Row Cottage, Rhu, on 20 May 1870 at Eliza's home. The wedding was conducted by Rev John Arthur, minister of Rhu Parish Church of Scotland; the witnesses were James Parlane and William Smith.

William and Eliza had five known children in Rhu; William (b. ~1873), Frederic (b. ~1875), Alexander (b. 9 July 1876), Edith (b. ~1879) and Sarah (b. ~1881). Son Alexander Parlane was born on 9 July 1876 at Glebeside Row, Rhu. In 1881, William Parlane, 39, a gardener, resided at Laurel Cottage, Rhu, with wife Eliza, 27, children William, 8, and Frederic, 6, both scholars, Alexander, 4, Edith, 2, and Sarah, 3 months old. William, a gardener, and wife Eliza were still alive in 1904.

Derek's paternal great-grandparents – John McKenzie and Margaret Chalmers

Derek's other paternal great-grandfather John McKenzie was born around 1838 in Alvah, Banffshire, to father John McKenzie, a farmer, and mother Eliza Kirkton. His great-grandmother Margaret Chalmers was born around 1843 in Alvah, Banffshire, to father John Chalmers, a crofter, and mother Jean Stewart. John McKenzie, 22, a farmer's son, of Coldhome, Alvah, married Margaret Chalmers, 17, of Muiryhill, Alvah, on 25 August 1860 at the Manse of Ord, Banff. The wedding was conducted by Rev James S Cassie, minister of Ord Church of Scotland; the witnesses were John Chalmers, Margaret's father, and James Chalmers, her brother. Daughter Isabella Bruce McKenzie was born around 1888 in Alvah. John, a farmer, was still alive in 1904, although, wife Margaret was dead by then.

Derek's maternal great-grandparents – Thomas Russell and Elizabeth George

Derek's maternal great-grandfather Thomas Russell and his great-grandmother Elizabeth George were born around 1866 in County Down, Ireland. Thomas Russell, an iron moulder, married Elizabeth George in the Presbyterian Church and they had two known children in Belfast, County Antrim; Catherine (b. ~1894) and Frank (b. ~1897). Elizabeth was dead by 1909 and Thomas had remarried second wife Sarah Jane McKnight by then. Thomas and Sarah Jane had a son John McKnight Russell (b. ~1910) in Belfast.

In 1911, Thomas Russell, 45, an iron moulder, resided at 13 Glencairn Street, Shankhill, Belfast, with wife Sarah Jane, 37, children Catherine, 17, a seamstress, Frank, 14, an assistant pawnbroker, and John McKnight, 9 months old. The family were Presbyterian and the Shankhill area of West Belfast was renowned for being staunchly Protestant and politically Unionist. In 1912, in opposition to the British Government's contentious Home Rule Parliament Act, most Ulster Protestant men signed the Ulster Covenant, including Thomas Russell of 25 Glencairn Street, Belfast at St Matthew's Parochial Hall, North Belfast, on Ulster Day, 28 September 1912.

Derek's maternal great-grandparents – Robert Caulfield and Margaret Nicholl

Derek's other maternal great-grandfather Robert Caulfield was born around 1869 in Bangor, County Down, Ireland, and his great-grandmother Margaret Nicholl was born around 1875 in County Antrim, Ireland. Robert Caulfield, a general contractor, married Margaret Nicholl and they had six known children in Bangor; Robert (b. ~1895), Sarah (b. ~1896), James (b. ~1899), Isabella (b. ~1903), John (b. ~1905) and Harriet (b. ~1907). In 1911, Robert Caulfield, a general contractor, resided at 28 Albert Street, Bangor, Down, with wife Margaret, 36, children Robert, 16, Sarah, 15, and James, 12, Isabella, 8, John, 6, all scholars, and Harriet, 4.

Derek's paternal great-great-grandparents – James Parlane and Agnes Wilson Smith

Derek's paternal great-great-grandfather James Parlane and great-great-grandmother Agnes Wilson Smith were both born around 1815 in Dunbartonshire. James Parlane, a calico printer, married Agnes Wilson Smith and they had a son William Parlane (b. 1 February 1841) in Alexandria, parish of Bonhill, Dunbartonshire. The birth is recorded in the OPRs for the parish of Bonhill as follows:-

> *OPR Births Bonhill 493/3/51*
> *1841: Parlane: William lawful son of James Parlane and Agnes Smith in Alexandria born 1ˢᵗ February 1841*

James, a calico printer, and Agnes were still alive in 1870 in Alexandria. Calico is a type of woven cotton cloth, coarser than muslin but finer than denim. In the mid-19th century, the small towns of Alexandria and Bonhill were centres of calico print works due to its plentiful supply of water from the River Leven. Alexandria, a town in Bonhill parish, Dunbartonshire, on the right bank of the Leven, opposite Bonhill town, with which it is connected by an iron suspension bridge of 438 feet span, erected in 1836. From a clachan or 'grocery', Alexandria has risen in less than a century to a busy and prosperous town, this rise was due to the bleaching, printing, and dyeing works established in the Vale of Leven since 1768. Alexandria contained one extensive calico print-work and Turkey-red dye work, and a clog and block factory.

Derek's paternal great-great-grandparents – Timothy John Walker and Mary Gill

Derek's other paternal great-great-grandfather Timothy John Walker was born in 1822 in Strood, Rochester, Kent, to father Thomas William Walker and mother Sarah Ann Townley. His great-great-grandmother Mary Gill was born in 1824 in Broadstairs, Kent. The National Archives holds a Merchant Navy Seamen's Record showing that Timothy Walker born Kent was enlisted for military service from 1845-54. Timothy John Walker, a sea captain, married wife Mary Gill on New Year's Day, 1 January 1848 in the Anglican Church at St Peter in Thanet, Broadstairs, Kent. Timothy and Mary had ten known children including; Eliza Ann (b. ~1853, Bromley, Middlesex), Emily Ann (b. ~1856), Alice Jane (b. ~1858), Amy (b. ~1860), a daughter (b. 1862,

Rhu), a daughter (b. 1863, Rhu), a son (b. 1864, Rhu), Henry (b. 14 February 1866, Rhu), Anne (b. 7 June 1867, Rhu) and Sarah (b. 20 April 1868, Rhu).

Timothy's naval role at Rhu was almost certainly as a training master for boys wishing to enter the naval services. The first naval training ship moored off Kidston Point near Rhu in the Gareloch was HMS Cumberland constructed in 1842. In 1869 she was converted for use as a training vessel by the Clyde Industrial Training Ship Association. The aim was to provide education and training for boys who, through poverty, neglect, or being orphaned, were destitute, homeless, and in danger of falling into vice or crime. Originally, boys were trained for entry into both the Royal Navy and the Merchant Service. However, after the Royal Navy decided to accept only boys of good character, the training became more orientated towards the Merchant Navy. Timothy, a sea captain in the Merchant Service, and wife Mary were still alive in 1870 in Rhu.

Derek's paternal great-great-grandparents – John McKenzie and Eliza Kirkton

Derek's other paternal great-great-grandfather John McKenzie and great-great-grandmother Eliza Kirkton were both born around 1810 in Banffshire. John McKenzie, a farmer, married Eliza Kirkton and they had two known sons John (b. ~1838) and James in Alvah, Banffshire. John, a farmer, and Eliza were still alive in 1860.

Derek's paternal great-great-grandparents – John Chalmers and Jean Stewart

Derek's other paternal great-great-grandfather John Chalmers and great-great-grandmother Jean Stewart were both born around 1815 in Banffshire. John Chalmers, a crofter, married Jean Stewart and they had a daughter Margaret (b. ~1843) in Alvah, Banffshire. John, a crofter, and Jean were still alive in 1860.

Derek's paternal great-great-great-grandparents – Thomas William Walker and Sarah Ann Townley

Derek's paternal great-great-great-grandfather Thomas William Walker was baptized on 11 April 1790 in Strood, Kent, England, and his great-great-great-grandmother Sarah Ann Townley were born on 7 January 1794 in Trench, Shropshire, England. Thomas William Walker married Sarah Ann Townley and they had a son Timothy John Walker (b. 1822) in Strood, Rochester, Kent. Thomas and Sarah Ann were still alive in 1861 in Bromley, Middlesex.

CONCLUSION

First and foremost, this book is a celebration of the achievement of a group of 15 young Scottish lads and one young German who, 48 years ago on 24 May 1972, achieved the extraordinary feat of winning the European Cup Winners' Cup, the first Scottish team to do so. Only one other Scottish side, Aberdeen, managed by the legendary Sir Alex Ferguson, has emulated this feat by beating Real Madrid 2-1 on 11 May 1983 in Gothenburg and possibly that story is for another book in the Pride series.

The family histories of the Scottish players wholly underlines the humbleness of their ancestral origins. These were men and women who crisscrossed Scotland to scratch a meagre living as agricultural labourers, coal miners, seamen, shipyard workers and domestic servants throughout the Dickensian Victorian era.

Into the 20th century, the family histories tell of the struggle to survive during two devastating world wars and the desperate poverty during the Great Depression of the 1930s. In many ways, the family histories of these men and women are no different from our family histories. Most of us can trace our ancestry back to humble beginnings throughout the agricultural and industrial revolutions. What defines this book is the culmination of these specific family histories in producing 16 remarkable young men who went on to create what was one of the great Scottish sporting achievements of the 20th century.

In conclusion, this book celebrates – the Barça Bears.

Player References

Sandy: The Authorised Biography of Sandy Jardine,
Tom Miller, 2016

John Greig: My Story, John Greig, 2006

DJ: The Derek Johnstone Story, Derek Johnstone &
Darrell King, 2007

Football in the Blood: My Autobiography,
Tommy McLean, 2013

Shooting Star: the Colin Stein Story, Colin Stein &
Paul Smith, 2009

Doddie: My Autobiography, Alex MacDonald, 2012

On the Wing: Willie Johnston, Willie Johnston, 1983

Genealogical References

National Records of Scotland, General Register House, Edinburgh

ScotlandsPeople.gov.uk

Association of Scottish Genealogists and Researchers in
Archives (ASGRA)

FamilySearch.org

Freebmd.org.uk

Census of Ireland: National Archives of Ireland

Ulster Covenant: PRONI, Public Records Office Northern
Ireland

Banffshire, the People and the Lands, Bruce B Bishop
ASGRA, 2009

Croft Histories of South Uist, Bill Lawson ASGRA, 1990

County Directory for Scotland, 1857

Pomphrey's Directory of Wishaw and Cambusnethan, 1893

British-genealogy.com

Online and Other References

The Mitchell Library

National Library of Scotland

National Archives, Kew, London

ScotlandsPlaces.gov.uk

Rangers.co.uk

Raithrovers.net

Londonhearts.org

The Scotsman

Canmore.org.uk

Wikipedia.co.uk

British Listed Buildings

Surname Database

Footballdatabase.eu

Fitbastats.com/Rangers

Ordnance Gazetteer of Scotland, Frances Broome, 1882-84

Football, Migration, and Industrial Patronage in the West of Scotland, c. 1870-1900, Sport in History, Matthew Lynn McDowell, 2012

Scotlandswar.co.uk/training_ships

Mannerstons.co.uk

rcdai.org.uk/priests-of-south-uist

Sir William Wallace, Geddes and Grosset, 2000

Glossary of Players' Origin of Surnames

Chapter 1: McCloy – a surname of Gaelic origin generally believed to be derived from 'Mac Lugaidh' meaning the 'son of Lewis'.

Chapter 2: Jardine – an Old French topographical or a vocational surname derived from 'jardin' meaning a garden.

Chapter 3: Mathieson – a Scottish patronymic surname of Biblical origin meaning 'the son of Matthew'.

Chapter 4: Greig – a diminutive surname of Gregory and Greek origin, from Gregorios meaning 'watchful' and later in Latin Gregorius associated with 'The Good Shepherd'.

Chapter 5: Johnstone – a Scottish locational surname believed to derive from the Norman held lands of Johnstone in Dumfriesshire, the original overlord granted lands there was named Jonis and thus the homesteading became known as 'Jonis toun'.

Chapter 6: Smith – recorded in the spellings of Smith, Smithe and Smythe this is the most popular surname in the English speaking world. Of pre-7th century Anglo-Saxon origin, it derives from the word 'smitan' meaning 'to smite' and as such is believed to have described not a blacksmith, but a soldier, one who smote. As he also wore armour, which he would have been required to repair, it may have led to the secondary meaning, i.e., that of a blacksmith.

Chapter 7: McLean – this notable surname, with spellings of MacLean, Maclean, MacLaine, McLean, McClean, McLane, etc., is widely recorded in Scotland and Ireland. It is a developed form of the Old Gaelic name 'Mac Gille Eoin', which translates as 'the son of the devotee of St John', from 'Mac', meaning son of, and 'gille', literally a servant or follower, and the saint's name 'Eoin' or 'Ian', the classic Gaelic form of John.

Chapter 8: Conn – an Anglicized form of the old Scots Gaelic 'Siol Cuin' or 'Con', literally meaning 'the seed or race of Con', a byname from the Gaelic 'con', a hound.

Chapter 9: Stein – in Scotland this is both a surname which derives either from a local dialectal form of the personal name Steven (from the Greek 'Stephanos' meaning 'laurel wreath') or from the Norse 'sten' - a stone. In Colin Stein's case, it is more likely from Steven.

Chapter 10: MacDonald – the derivation is from the Gaelic 'Mac Dhomhnuill', translating as 'son of Donald'. It is said that the personal name 'Donald' translates as 'world-rule' alluding to the clan's title of Lord of the Isles.

Chapter 11: Johnston – a Scottish locational surname believed to derive from the Norman held lands of Johnstone in Dumfriesshire, the original overlord granted lands there was named Jonis and thus the homesteading became known as 'Jonis toun'.

Chapter 12: Neef – a surname of Dutch / German origin derived from the meaning of 'nephew'.

Chapter 13: Denny – in this instance this name is almost certainly a Scottish locational surname after Denny in Stirlingshire.

Chapter 14: Fyfe – another Scottish locational surname after the Kingdom of Fife, which might derive from the meaning of 'a windy place'.

Chapter 15: Penman – of Old French origin and derives from the word 'paniere' and was introduced by the Normans. It usually described a maker of baskets or pans, but in England was almost certainly a vocational surname for a hawker, one who travelled carrying his or her goods in panniers.

Chapter 16: Parlane – it originates from the Gaelic 'Mac Pharlain', meaning 'son of Parlan', a name which derives from the Greek 'Partalan' a patronymic form of the Biblical name 'Bartholomew'.

Glossary of Key Names

Chapter 1: Peter McCloy

Allwell, Isabella
Allwell, Janet
Allwell, Janet
Allwell, Peter
Allwell, Peter Sr.
Duff, Sarah Jane
Edgar, Jane
Faulds, William
Gillies, Janet
Goodfellow, Rev R K
Goram, Andy
Hendrie, Rev George S
Jamieson, James
Kane, Mary McGilp
Kennedy, Stewart
Leighton, Jim
Lyon, Alexander
Lyon, Elizabeth McConnochie
Lyon, John
Lyon, Mary McGilp
Lyon, Mary McWhirter
Lyon, Thomas
Lyon, Thomas Sr.
McCloy, Andrew
McCloy, David
McCloy, David Sr.
McCloy, Ellen
McCloy, Henry
McCloy, Henry
McCloy, James
McCloy, James Sr.
McCloy, Jeanie
McCloy, Peter Allwell Lyon
McFarlane, Esquire
McFarlane, Janet
McGilp, Archibald
McGilp, Isabella

McGilp, Janet
McGilp, Mary
McWhirter, Jane
Minto, Rev Patrick Wood
Moore, James
Shearer, Jane
Souness, Graeme
Stewart, Jim
Stokes, Helen
Stokes, Joseph
Thom, Agnes
Thom, Agnes Cron
Thom, Duncan
Thom, Janet
Thom, Jeanie
Thom, John
Thom, Maggie
Thom, Mary Bell
Waddell, Willie
Wallace, Jock
White, Rev Samuel
Wilson, Mary

Chapter 2: Sandy Jardine

Alexander, George C
Ballantyne, Robert
Buchanan, Peter
Duffy, Celia
Haig, Earl Douglas
Haig, James
Haig, John Richard
Heron, Agnes
Jardine, David J
Jardine, David
Jardine, James
Jardine, James Jr.
Jardine, James Sr.
Jardine, Marion Lithgow
Jardine, Robert
Jardine, William

Jardine, William Sr.
Jardine, William Pullar
Laidlaw, Elizabeth
Laidlaw, William
Lithgow, Marion
Lithgow, Robert
Man, Joseph
McClelland, Rev Robert S
McCoist, Ally
McLoan, Emily
McWilliam, Agnes
Menelaws, Agnes
Menelaws, Alexander
Menelaws, George
Menelaws, George Sr.
Menelaws, Georgina
Menelaws, James
Menelaws, James Sr.
Menelaws, Margaret Laidlaw
Menelaws, Violet
Menelaws, William
Menelaws, William Sr.
Paxton, Elizabeth
Pevay, Elizabeth
Pirie, Margaret G
Porter, Fr David B
Pullar, Ann
Pullar, David
Pullar, James Ross
Pullar, Margaret Perry
Pullar, William
Pullar, William Sr.
Ross, Finlay
Ross, Mary
Smith, Margaret
Smith, Rev Andrew M
Smith, Rev W Whyte
Stewart, Janet
Tasker, Rev W
Walkinshaw, Violet

Wallace, Jock
White, Davie

Chapter 3:
Willie Mathieson

Aitken, George
Anderson, Elizabeth
Anderson, Helen
Arnott, Helen
Black, Ann
Black, James
Black, Margaret
Cameron, Rev Allan
Campbell, Andrew
Campbell, Janet
Campbell, Margaret
Dewar, Annie
Dewar, George
Douglas, Rev Donald H
Fleming, D.
Forsyth, Tam
Grant, Rev Patrick McGregor
Halkett, Annie
Heaton, Ann
Horn, Werner
Houston, Rev A McNeil
MacGregor, D.
Mathewson, Andrew
Mathewson, David
Mathewson, Janet
Mathewson, John
Mathewson, Margaret
Mathewson, William
Mathieson, Andrew
Mathieson, Robert
Mathieson, William
Mathieson, William Sr.
McGregor, Alexander
McGregor, Elizabeth
McMillan, Janet

Chapter 4: John Greig

Chapter 5: Derek Johnstone

Gow, Fr William C

Grant, Isobel

Grant, Margaret

Henry, D J Procurator Fiscal

Hughson, Emily Elizabeth Perry

Hughson, Magnus William

Jackson, Colin

Johnstone, Derek Joseph

Johnstone, James

Johnstone, James Forsyth

Johnstone, James Joseph

Johnstone, James Sr.

Johnstone, Joseph

Johnstone, Ronald

Keenan, Mary

Kinnear, Dr Peter MB ChB

Logan, Rev J Victor

Macintyre, Alexander

Macintyre, Annie

Macintyre, Donald

Macintyre, Jane

Macintyre, John

McGuckin, Charles

McKimmie, Alexander

McKimmie, William

McKinnon, Ronnie

McLean, Jim

McPherson, Sarah

Paterson, Elspeth Helen

Rae, Alexander

Ritchie, Mary Ann

Rose, Joseph

Russell, Mary

Short, Christina Jamieson McIntosh

Short, Margaret

Souness, Graeme

Steele, Norman

Sutherland, Rev Andrew N

Turner, Dr A. MD

Wallace, Jock

Wilson, Rev John

Chapter 6:
Dave Smith

Baigrie, Hugh Wallace

Baigrie, Isabella

Baigrie, Margaret Collie Burness

Baigrie, William

Barron, Helen Findlay

Barron, Margaret

Barron, William

Burness, Alexander

Burness, Alexander Sr.

Burness, Margaret Cruikshank

Burns, Robert

Cameron, John

Collie, Annie Caie

Collie, Catherine

Collie, Margaret

Collie, Peter Beattie

Collie, Sam

Collie, Samuel

Cox, Rev J T

Cruikshank, Margaret

Cumming, Jane

Dalgarno, Rev James

Damean, Rev John

Findlay, Helen

Keith, Helen Y

Macintyre, John

Mearns, James Watt

Millar Rev PC

Milne, Ann

Simpson, Mary

Simpson, Robert

Smith, David Bruce

Smith, Doug

Smith, Hugh

Smith, James Henry

Smith, Jean

Chapter 7: Tommy McLean

Chapter 8: Alfie Conn

Edmond, William

Ewing, Janet

Ewing, Matthew

Fergus, Fr M. MA

Finlayson, Jane

Goldberg, Dr Hans C. MB

Goodfellow, Margaret Finlayson

Goodfellow, Marion

Goodfellow, Peter

Greenlees, Jane

Hotchkiss, Hannah

Hotchkiss, William

Irvine, William

Jones, Rev Cyril

Laing, E.

Laing, John

MacLennan, Rev Kenneth

McDonald, Dr James MB CM

Nicholson, Bill

Storrie, Robert

Storrie, Susan

Thomson, Elizabeth

Thomson, Rev D L

Wardhaugh, Jimmy

Williams, Messrs J & Coy.

Wotherspoon, John

Chapter 9:
Colin Stein

Anderson, Colin Thompson

Anderson, Edith

Anderson, Helen Scott

Anderson, John

Anderson, John Sr.

Anthony, David

Anthony, Elizabeth

Ball, D K

Ball, John

Ball, Mary McMeeking

Baul, John

Baul, Joseph

Campbell, Rev A D

Charles, Rev James

Cross, Dr Robert MB CM

Crozier, David

Dalyell, General Tam

Dalyell, Tam MP

Dalyell, Thomas

Emslie, Elizabeth

Kelly, Mary

Laurie, Robina

Meldrum, James of the Bynnis

Oliphant, Rev Johnston

Paris, Christina Black

Paris, Elizabeth

Paris, James

Paris, Mary

Paris, William

Scott, Helen

Scott, Margaret

Stein, Alexander

Stein, Alexander Sr.

Stein, Bobby

Stein, Christina Paris

Stein, Colin Anderson

Stein, David

Stein, Elizabeth

Stein, Ellen

Stein, George

Stein, Henry

Stein, James

Stein, John

Stein, Peter

Stein, Robert Scott

Stein, William

Stein, William Jr.

Swords, William

Thom, Dr R B MB ChB

Thomson, Agnes

Waddell, Willie

Wardrop, Rev James
White, Davie

Chapter 10:
Alex MacDonald

Bonaparte, Napoleon
Brown, Margaret
Campbell, Ann
Campbell, Christina
Campbell, Donald
Campbell, Marion
Campbell, Mrs Ann
Carlin, Margaret Brown
Carlin, Thomas
Cryans, Agnes
Cryans, John
Docherty, Marion
Docherty, Sarah
Fleming, Fr Charles E
MacColl, Fr Donald
MacDonald, Alexander
MacDonald, Alexander Sr.
MacDonald, Angus
MacDonald, Angus Sr. (1)
MacDonald, Angus Sr. (2)
MacDonald, Ann
MacDonald, Bishop Angus
MacDonald, Donald
MacDonald, Donald Jr.
MacDonald, Donald Sr.
MacDonald, Euphemia
MacDonald, Flora
MacDonald, John
MacDonald, Marshal Etienne J J A
MacEachan, Neil of Howbeg
Macintyre, Donald
MacKay, Rev John
McDonald, Dr L. LRCP
McLellan, Archibald
McLellan, Catherine

Morrison, Kate
O'Neil, Margaret
Shannon, Annie
Shannon, Thomas
Stewart, Prince Charles Edward
Todd, Pastor Thomas
Walker, Margaret
Wallace, Daniel
Watson, Adam
Watson, Agnes
Watson, Janet C.
Watson, Robert
White, Davie

Chapter 11:
Willie Johnston

Aitken, Agnes
Anderson, Christina
Anderson, Elizabeth
Anderson, James
Anderson, John
Anderson, John Sr.
Anderson, Lilias
Anderson, Marion
Anderson, Mary
Anderson, William Johnstone
Brown, John & Coy.
Clarke, Alexander
Clarke, Mary Ann
Copland, Elizabeth
Copland, Isabella
Copland, Mary
Copland, William
Copland, William Johnstone
Costley, Rosina
Costley, William
Crawford, Marion
Exelby, Mary Ann Dowson
Exelby, William Thomson
Fraser, Alexander

Garrity, Bella
Garrity, John
Garrity, Mary Jane
Green, Rev George G.
Harrison, Mary Ann
Harrison, Valentine
Hirohito, Emperor
Imrie, Dr J A MD
Johnston, Essie
Johnston, William
Johnston, William Copland
Johnston, William McClure
Lamont, Rev M.
MacLeod, Ally
McClure, Catherine
McClure, George
McClure, Helen
McClure, Henry Robert
McClure, Holt
McClure, Margaret Jane
McClure, Valentine
McClure, William
McClure, William Henry
McDonald, John
Rankin, Catherine
Ritchie, David
Ritchie, Isabella Gordon
Smith, William
Taylor, Rev George W
Thomson, Rev Robert
Trainer, Helen
Wilson, Davie

Chapter 12: Gerry Neef

Martin, Norrie
Neef, Klaus Gerhard
Neef, Oliver
Neef, Paul
Neef, Wolfgang
Ritchie, Billy

Schultes, Emma
Turnbull, Eddie
Tyson, Maria Frances
Waddell, Willie
White, Davie
Wilhelm, Kaiser

Chapter 13: Jim Denny

Alexander, E.
Bickerstaff, Henry
Blind Harry
Brown, Alexander
Brown, Annie
Coats, J & P Ltd.
Craig, Susan
Davidson, Fr William
Denny, David
Denny, Duncan
Denny, Duncan Sr.
Denny, James
Denny, James Jr.
Denny, James Sr.
Denny, M.
Donnelly, Jeanie
Farmer, Michael
Ferguson, Jane
Flanagan, Mary Ann
Gilchrist, Margaret
Gilchrist, Robert
Kelly, Rev G J Davidson
McGrory, Mary
McIndoe, Rev W.
McLeod, Elizabeth
McNeil, Mary
Merrylees, Rev C J T
Morrison, A.
Niven, Rev Frederick Charles
Quail, Elizabeth
Quail, Mary Thomas Lauchlan
Quail, Thomas Andrew

Quail, William
Somerville, Jeanie
Stewart, A.
Thomas, Margaret
Wallace, David
Wallace, Jeanie McLeod
Wallace, Sir William

O'Neill, Nellie
O'Neill, Susan Beck
O'Neill. Patrick
Ogilvie, Jessie
Ogilvie, Susan

Wilkie, Rev Robert

Chapter 14: Graham Fyfe

Baird, William & Coy.
Beck, Annie
Bryson, Margaret
Caffrey, James
Crosbie, Isabella
Crosbie, James
Crosbie, James Sr.
Crosbie, Maud
Davie, Isabella
Fyfe, Alexander
Fyfe, Alexander Sr.
Fyfe, Graham Ellerby
Fyfe, Jane
Fyfe, William McKenzie
Fyfe, William McKenzie Sr.
Kennedy, Sarah
Leonard, Fr John
Macguire, Mary
McDonald, Alan
McGurk, Edward
McGurk, Ellen
McGurk, John
Murray, Fr Thomas J.
Murray, Rev John A.
O'Neill, Andrew
O'Neill, Edward
O'Neill, John
O'Neill, John Jr.
O'Neill, John Sr.
O'Neill, Maggie Bryson
O'Neill, Mary

Chapter 15: Andy Penman

Aitchison, John & Coy.
Aitchison, William & Coy.
Begg, Rev Dr.
Blackwood, Margaret
Bonar, Mary
Boyd, Rev Arnold
Calder, Helen
Duncan, Agnes
Duncan, Alexander
Duncan, Peter
Forbes, Charlotte Ann Tawse
Forbes, John Mack
Forbes, William James Hay
Gardiner, Rev Andrew
Gilzean, Alan
Hammond, Daniel Sr.
Hammond, Helen Calder
Hammond, Sergeant Daniel
Harrows, Maggie
Lintore, Dr John MD
MacDonald, Rev Charles Cadell
Main, James
Murray, Ann
Penman, Agnes
Penman, Andrew
Penman, Ann
Penman, Elizabeth
Penman, George
Penman, Helen
Penman, Helen Sr.
Penman, Hugh

Penman, James

Penman, James Jr.

Penman, James Sr. (1)

Penman, James Sr. (2)

Penman, Jane

Penman, Janet

Penman, Maggie

Penman, Margaret

Penman, Mary

Penman, Thomas

Penman, William

Penman, William Sr.

Riddell, James

Robertson, John

Sinclair, Rev James W.

Smith, Alexina Gordon

Smith, Ellen

Smith, James

Smith, James Riddell

Smith, Margaret

Smith, Rev David

Tawse, Margaret

Thomson, Margaret

Tulloch, Margaret

Tulloch, William

Turnbull, John

Turner, Dougal

Watson, Margaret

White, Davie

Wilson, Helen

Chapter 16:
Derek Parlane

Allan, Millie

Arthur, Rev John

Campbell, Peter

Cassie, Rev James S.

Caulfield, Harriet

Caulfield, Isabella

Caulfield, James

Caulfield, John

Caulfield, Robert

Caulfield, Robert Sr.

Caulfield, Sarah

Chalmers, James

Chalmers, John

Chalmers, Margaret

George, Elizabeth

Gill, Mary

Kirkton, Eliza

McBeath, William

McKenzie, Isabella Bruce

McKenzie, John

McKenzie, John Sr.

McKnight, John

McKnight, Sarah Jane

McNeil, Moses

McNeil, Peter

McNeill, Billy

Nicholl, Margaret

Parlane, Alexander

Parlane, Derek James

Parlane, Edith

Parlane, Frederic

Parlane, Ian

Parlane, James

Parlane, James Sr.

Parlane, Sarah

Parlane, William

Parlane, William Sr.

Robertson, William

Russell, Catherine

Russell, Frank

Russell, Margaret Nicholl

Russell, Thomas

Smith, Agnes Wilson

Smith, William

Stewart, Jean

Thornton, Willie

Tolmie, Jim
Townley, Sarah Ann
Waddell, Willie
Walker, Alice Jane
Walker, Amy
Walker, Anne
Walker, Captain Timothy John
Walker, Eliza Ann
Walker, Emily Ann
Walker, Henry
Walker, Sarah
Walker, Thomas William
Wilson, Rev James

ABOUT THE AUTHOR

Derek Niven is a pseudonym used by the author John McGee, a member of ASGRA, in the publication of his factual genealogical writings and Derek Beaugarde for his fictional science fiction writings. John McGee, aka 'The Two Dereks', was born in 1956 in the railway village of Corkerhill, Glasgow and he attended Mosspark Primary and Allan Glen's schools. The late great actor Sir Derek Bogarde spent two unhappy years at Allan Glen's when he was a pupil named Derek Niven van den Bogaerde, thus the observant reader will readily be able to discern the origin of the two pseudonyms. After spending 34 years in the rail industry in train planning and accountancy John McGee retired in 2007. In 2012 the idea for his apocalyptic science fiction novel first emerged and 2084: The End of Days © Derek Beaugarde was published by Corkerhill Press in 2016. This was followed by Pride of the Lions © Derek Niven published by Corkerhill Press in 2017 and Pride of the Jocks © Derek Niven, foreword by Kathleen Murdoch, published by Corkerhill Press in 2018.

By The Same Author

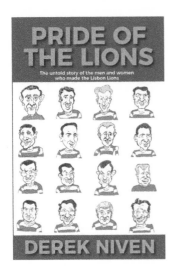

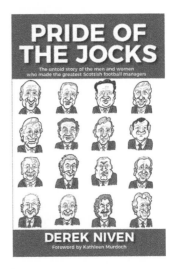

Writing as Derek Beaugarde

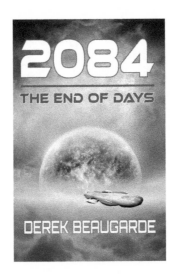